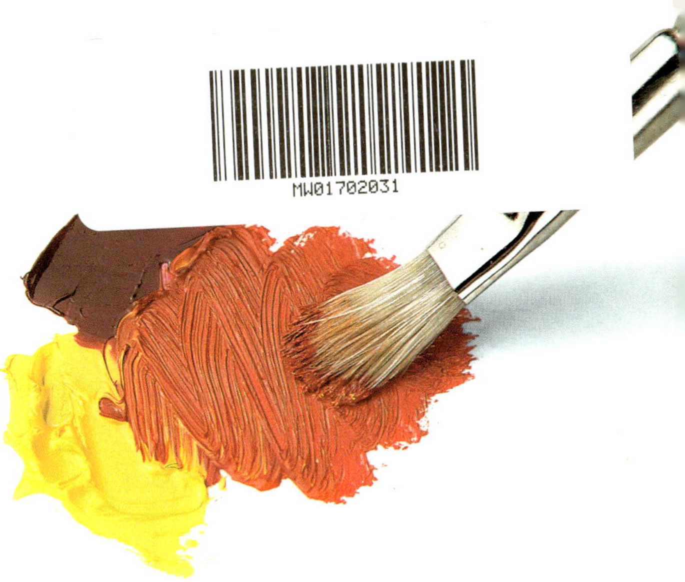

mixing colors: oils

Original title of the book in Spanish is *Para empezar a pintar: mezcla de colores óleo*

Published by Parramón Ediciones, S.A., Barcelona, Spain

Author: Parramón's Editorial Team
Illustrator: Parramón's Editorial Team

All inquiries should be addressed to:
Barron's Educational Series, Inc.
250 Wireless Boulevard
Hauppauge, New York 11788
http://www.barronseduc.com

Library of Congress Catalog Card No. 99-20235

International Standard Book No. 0-7641-0889-1

Library of Congress Cataloging-in-Publication Data
Para empezar a pintar mezcla de colores óleo. English.
Learning to paint, mixing colors—oils / [author, Parramón's Editorial Team ; illustrator, Parramón's Editorial Team].
p. cm. — (Barron's art guides)
ISBN 0-7641-0889-1
1. Color in art. 2. Painting—Technique. I. Parramón Ediciones. Editorial Team. II. Title. III. Series.
ND1488.P3413 1999
751.45—dc21 99-20235
CIP

Printed in Spain
9 8 7 6 5 4 3 2 1

BARRON'S ART GUIDES

LEARNING TO PAINT

mixing colors: oils

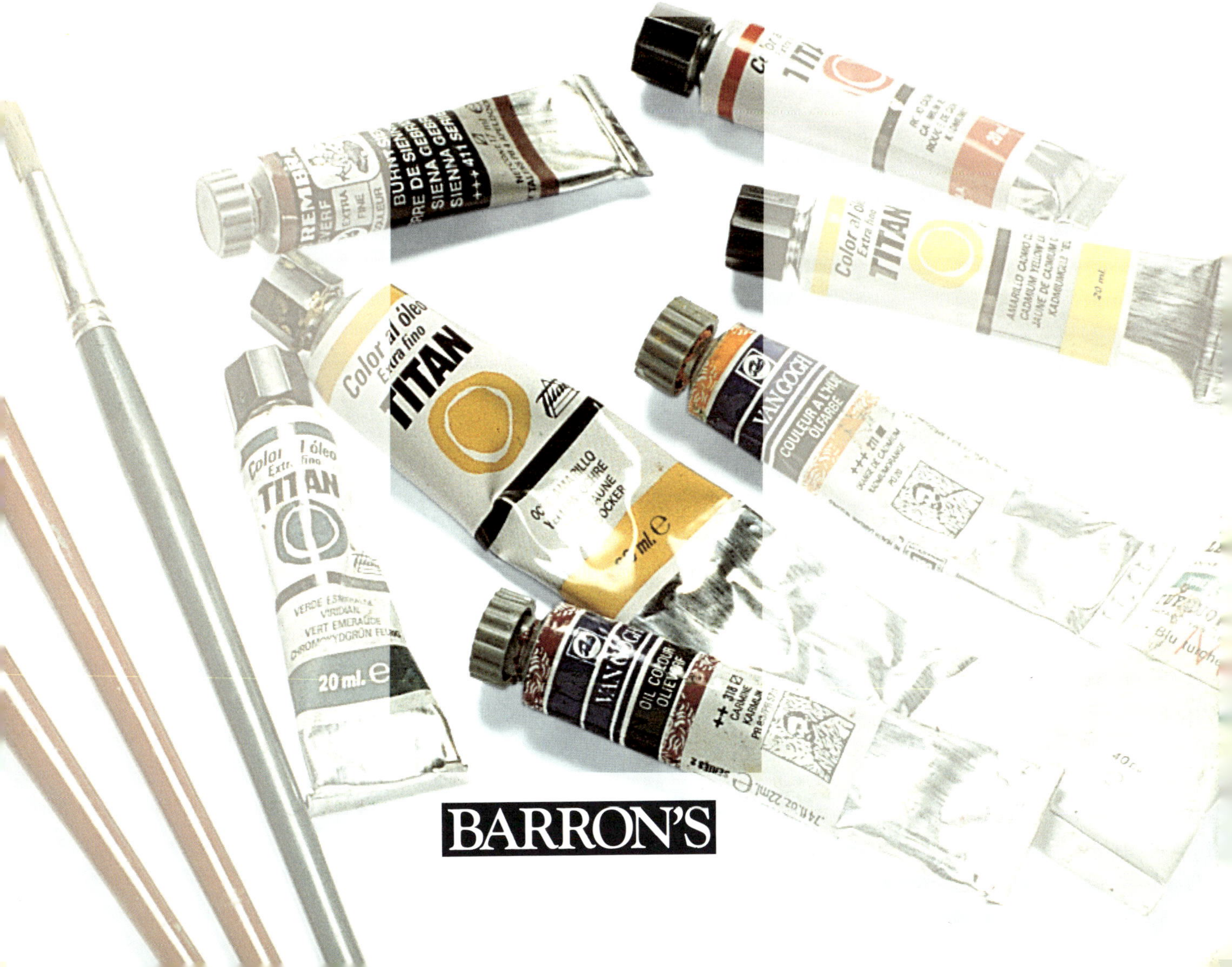

BARRON'S

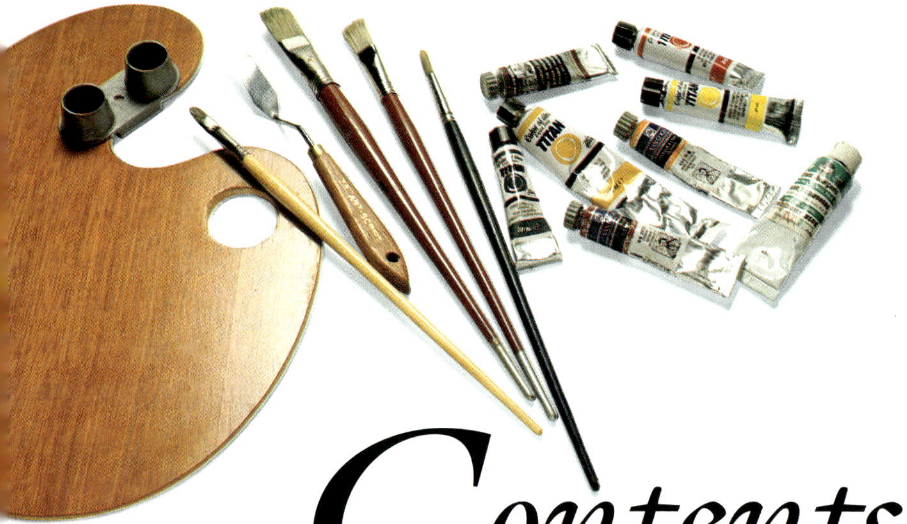

Contents

BASIC TECHNIQUES

BASIC EXERCISES

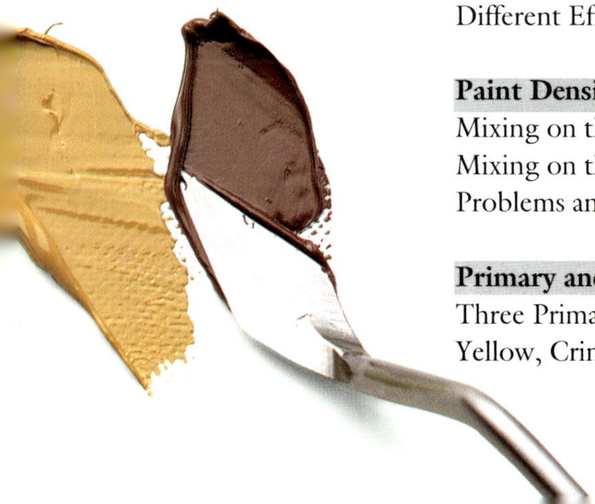

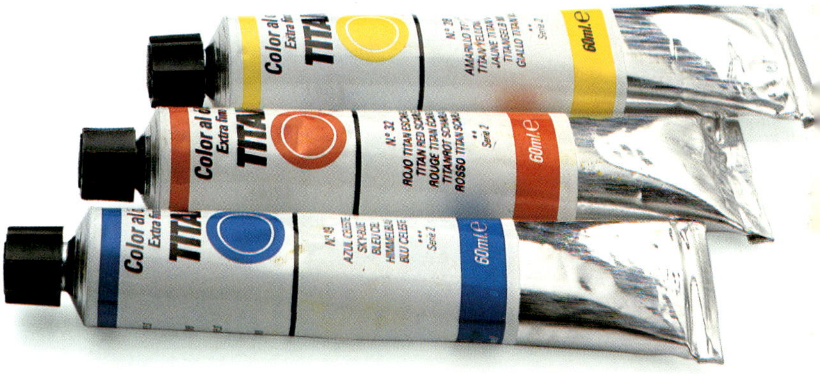

Oil painting is one of the most attractive painting mediums and the one with the most followers. Its extraordinary versatility makes it a fascinating medium. Oil paint can be worked in fine layers, like veils, or as a thick paste. It can also be applied wet over wet and dry over wet. Thus, techniques range through grading, blending, mottling, glazing, frottage, etc., creating many different finishes, from glossy and transparent to opaque and dull.

People who are interested in oil painting and who wish to try it out will find in these pages a compendium of knowledge, simple explanations, and practical exercises progressing in difficulty, all dealing with mixing colors.

The colors we see in nature are generally different from the oil paint that comes out of a tube. In order to paint from observation, the painter has to know how to mix the colors on the palette to achieve the hues that the eye sees.

The reader should not despair if unsuccessful at first try while carrying out an exercise. Every working artist knows that mistakes provide the best schooling and that it takes willpower to sustain the practice of painting.

This book is aimed at encouraging everybody who wishes to enter into the world of oil painting. The satisfaction found there is inexhaustible.

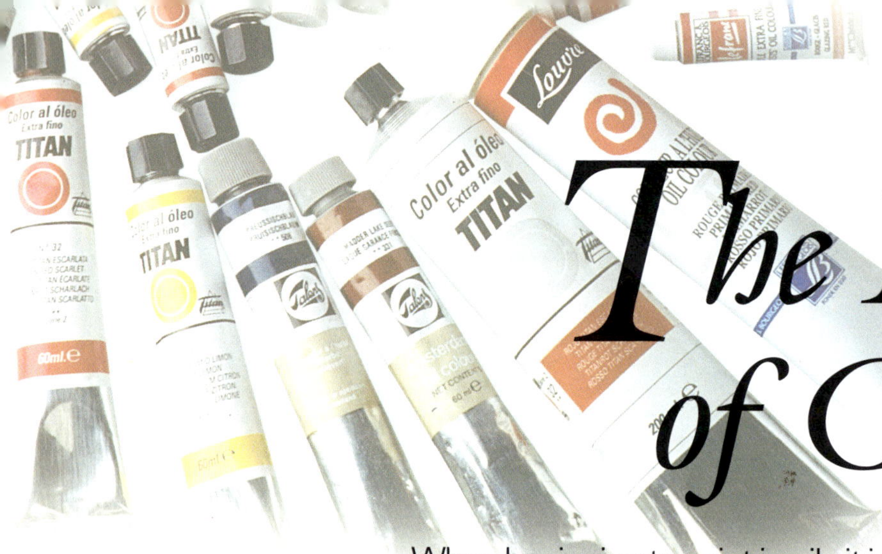

The Palette of Colors

When beginning to paint in oils it is best to start with a reduced number of colors on your palette. There are not many colors in the following group, but enough to produce all the mixtures you may need.

Titanium White
The oil painter needs white to mix with colors in order to obtain lighter shades. It is a good idea to buy the 1-pound tube of white since you will likely use more of it than any other color.

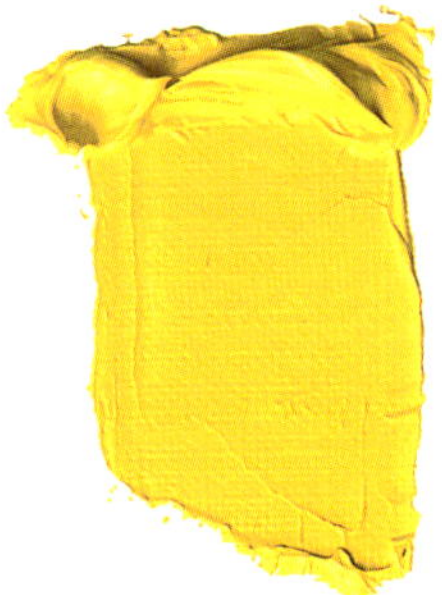

Cadmium Yellow Light
After white, this is the lightest and the brightest color on the palette. Yellow and white are the paints on your palette that are the slowest to dry. Cadmium Yellow Light is one of the three basic colors on this palette.

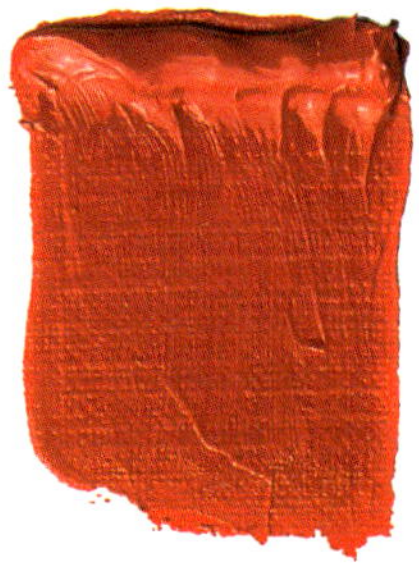

Vermilion
Among the range of red colors, vermilion is bright, a real red. Of the two reds on this palette, vermilion is the most opaque.

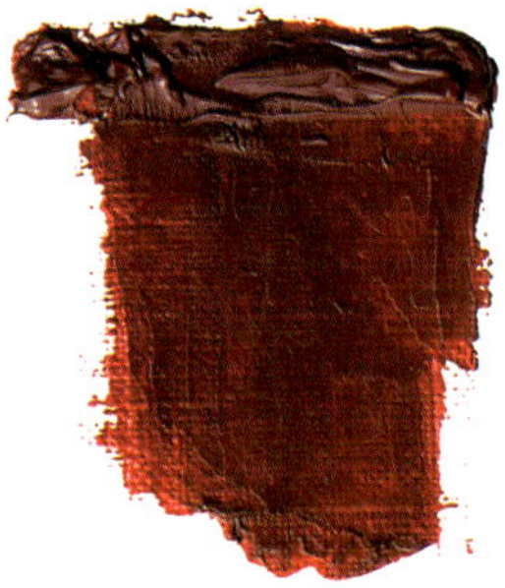

Alizarin Crimson
This is a very powerful red. Compared with vermilion, crimson is darker. When using crimson, bear in mind that this is a very transparent color.

REMEMBER...

- The word palette is used to refer to both the wooden, plastic, or ceramic implement, as well as the set of colors being used.
- The most practical colors, and the most widely used, are those sold in small, medium-sized, and large tubes.
- In addition to the oil paints used straight from the tube, other minimum essential colors will have to be mixed. A support, such as canvas, canvas board, or wood, and an easel are needed, together with palette, paintbrushes and palette knives, palette cups and solvents, and cotton rags and other cleaning articles.

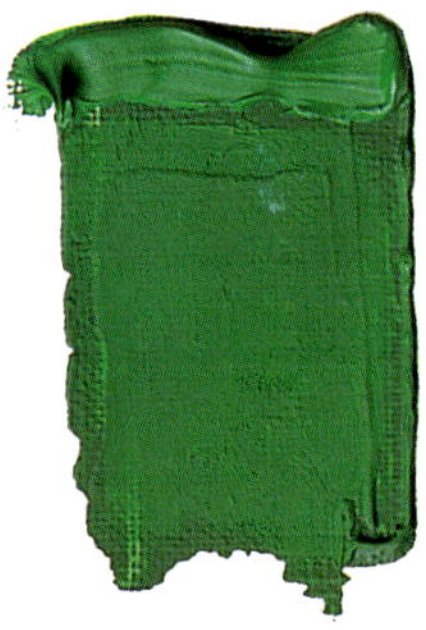

Permanent Green Light
Permanent Green Light is the lighter of the two greens on our palette. Its inclusion in this group of colors will help you to mix a whole range of greens and neutral colors.

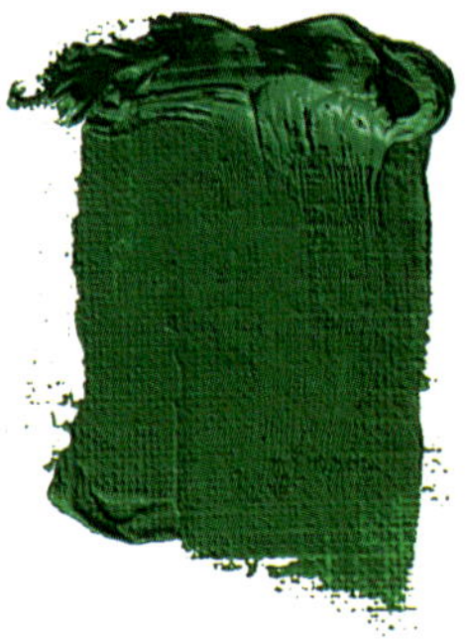

Chromium Oxide Green
Chromium Oxide Green is the dark green on your palette. Using a Chromium Oxide Green base, and mixing with other colors, practically any shade of green can be obtained.

Colors to Start Out With

The colors suggested cannot be too numerous or the beginning painter will get confused. At the same time, this palette must serve to mix all the hues that the painter may wish to reproduce. Another criterion for the selection of the colors recommended here is ease of handling when mixing. All throughout this book you will be introduced to the practice of mixing colors. After carrying out the exercises in this guide, you will know which colors have to be mixed and in what amounts.

Color Groups

There are several ways of classifying colors. At this point we can mention the so-called color groups. Colors can be grouped as follows: whites, yellows, reds, greens, blues, browns, and blacks.

This suggested palette includes a white, two yellows (yellow and ochre), three reds (vermilion, crimson, and burnt sienna), two greens, two blues, a brown (burnt umber), and a black. Colors can also be grouped according to their origins, as is the case with the earth colors, which include ochre, sienna, and umber.

Yellow Ochre
The yellowest of the earth colors, ochre is a golden color, duller and browner than cadmium yellow.

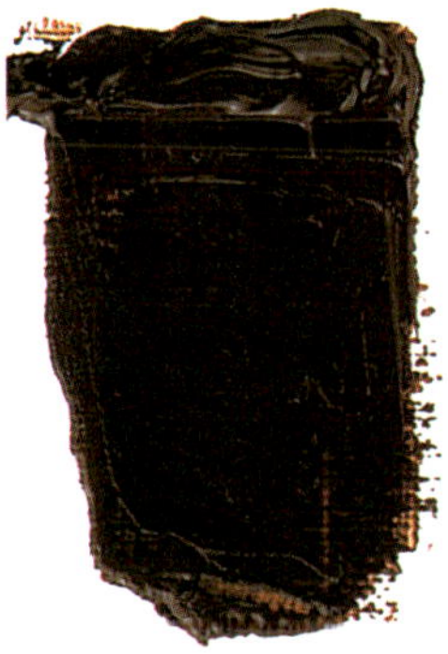

Burnt Sienna
The reddest of the earth colors. Compared with vermilion, it is a dull brownish red.

Burnt Umber
This is the darkest of the earth colors. As its name suggests, it is the somber color of the palette, very dark, almost black.

REMEMBER...

- This suggested palette will serve to begin with but, with practice, you will find that it is necessary to extend it.
- A lemon yellow and a medium yellow will give you the chance to create more and cleaner tones. By adding the "lakes" (such as Rose Lake) to the group of reds, mixtures of great chromatic intensity can be achieved. Among the blues, Prussian Blue, though very dark, will allow you to obtain much clearer blues, once you have some experience using it.

Winsor Blue
If you compare the blues we have suggested, Winsor Blue is the warmer and lighter of the two. Winsor Blue is the third basic color on the palette.

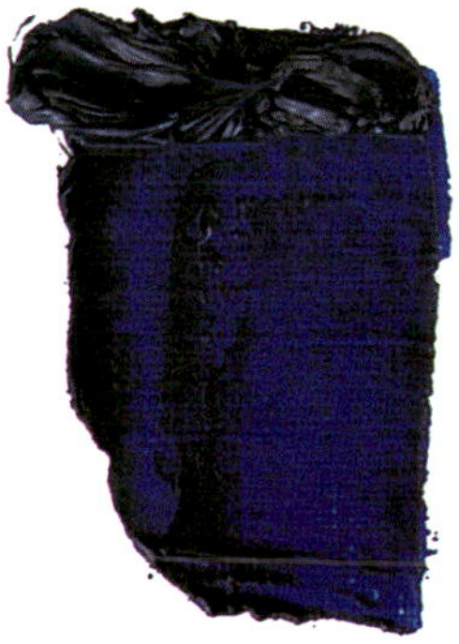

Ultramarine
This is the cooler and darker blue on the palette. If you observe it closely, you will recognize the violet tinge, so typical of ultramarine.

Ivory Black
Black appears on this page, and in successive exercises, but the beginner should take note that it should not be used for mixing, as it tends to dull color. We strongly recommend that, after completing the exercises in this guide, you consider working without this color in order to keep your colors rich and vibrant.

Mixing

Though the mixing of oil paints is done on the palette, colors are also adjusted on the canvas, over prepainted colors that are still wet. There are several procedures for which the painter can use a brush or a palette knife, although the fingers can also be used.

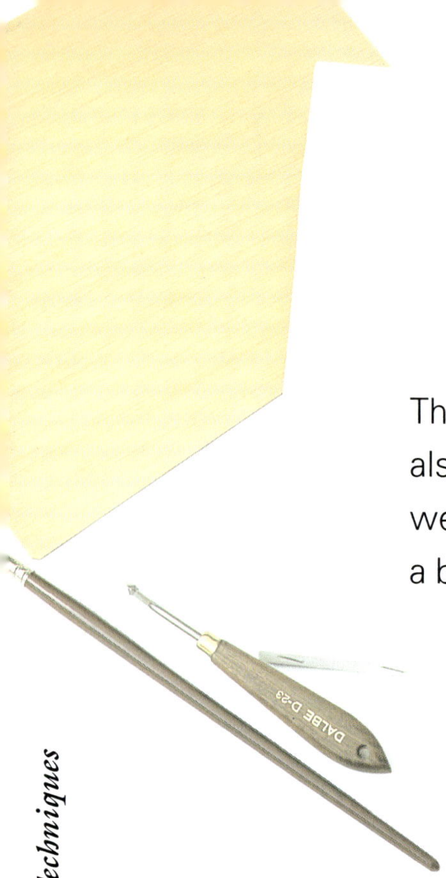

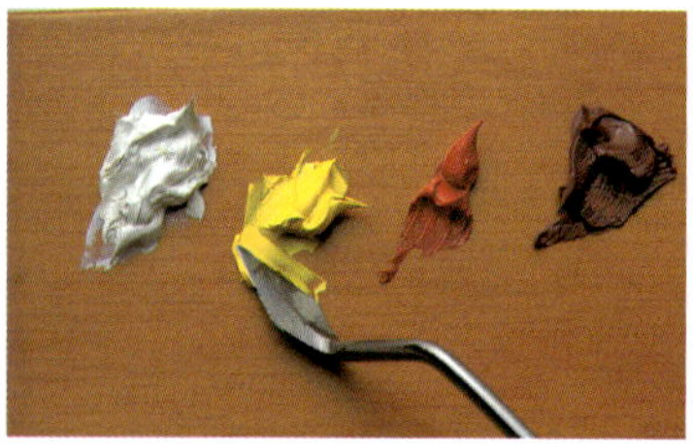

The palette knife is used to pick up paints that have been squeezed onto the palette from the tube, in preparation for mixing. Use it to pick up only the quantity needed.

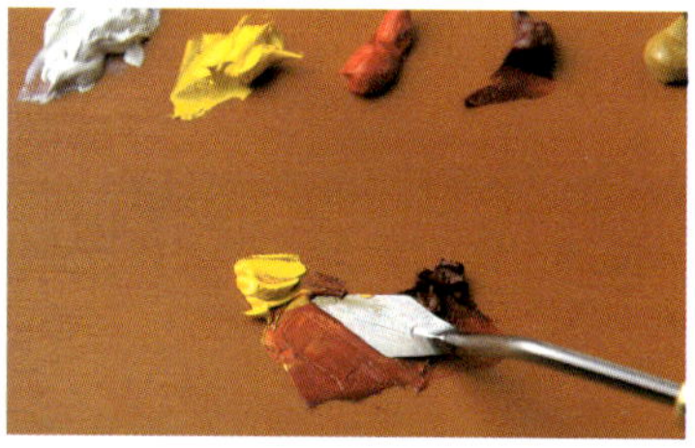

Previously separate colors can then be blended together with the palette knife. In general terms, the palette knife is used to both pick up and mix oil colors.

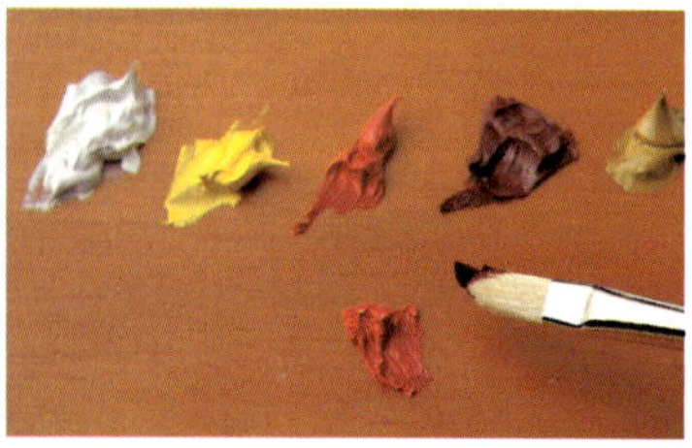

The colors for a mixture can also be brought to the mixing area on the palette using a paintbrush.

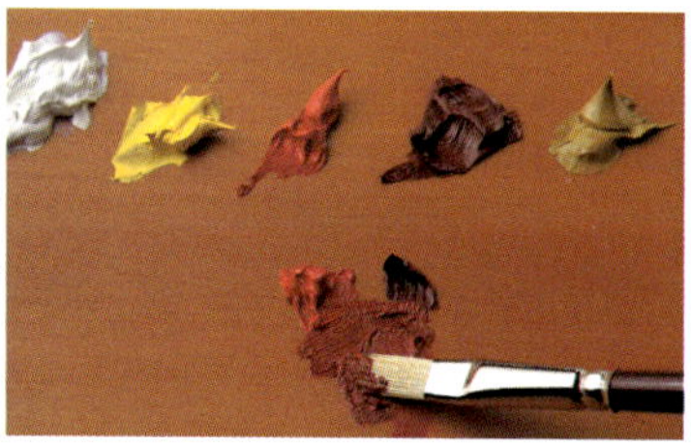

Paint can be picked up with a palette knife, then mixed with a paintbrush.

On the Palette

The palette has a thumb-hole that allows you to hold it in one hand while mixing colors and painting with the other. Mixture should be done on a clean area of the palette. For this reason, if, after a long work session, the palette becomes messy with mixtures, it will have to be cleaned with turpentine and paper towels.

First the bulk of paint remaining on the palette is removed with paper towel. Then, using more toweling or a cotton rag soaked in turpentine, the rest of the paint can be wiped away until the palette is clean.

REMEMBER...

- The palette, palette knives, and paintbrush are the essential tools for mixing oil paint.
- While the paint is still wet on the canvas, the mixtures can be varied and the color adjusted.

With a Palette Knife, with a Paintbrush

Both a palette knife and a paintbrush can be used for mixing, but the palette knife is more frequently used to mix large amounts of paint.

Both the shape of the palette knife and the size of the paintbrush depend on the painter's personal preference.

On the Canvas

Oil paint can also be mixed directly on canvas or other supports. The most common practice is that of working directly into colors that have already been applied, adjusting them with other colors or mixtures.

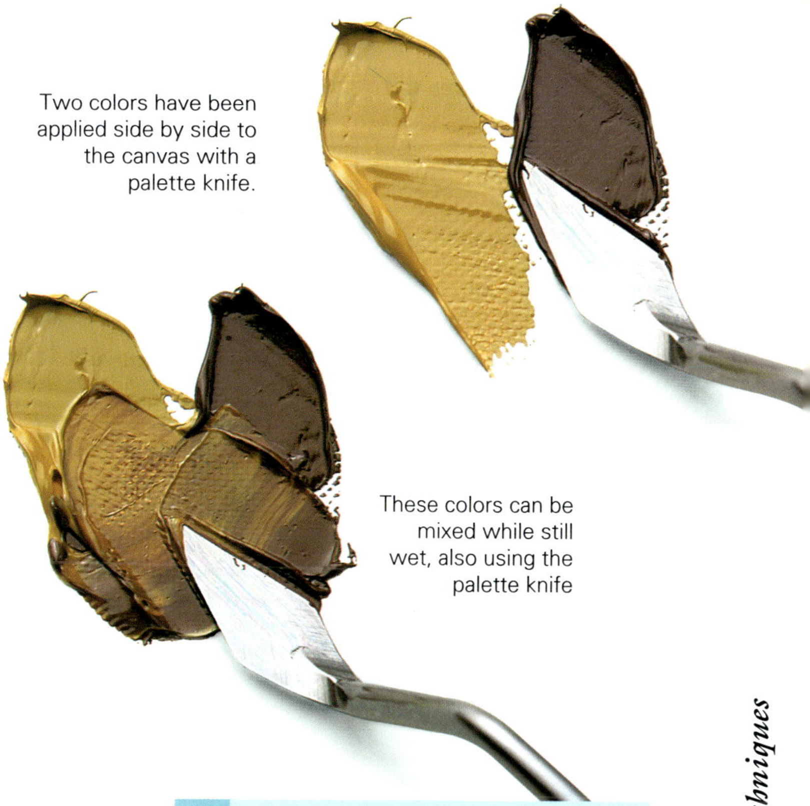

Two colors have been applied side by side to the canvas with a palette knife.

These colors can be mixed while still wet, also using the palette knife

With a Palette Knife, Paintbrush, and Finger

Both palette knives and paintbrushes can be used to apply the paint to the canvas. If these tools are heavily loaded with paint, thick impastos can be produced.

Besides the palette knife and the paintbrush, the hand can also be used to complete the mixture of colors on the canvas, blending the colors with the fingertip. This is done by pressing on the paint and rubbing downward or in circular movements. The resulting mixture is very uniform and produces a very interesting plastic effect. It is highly suited for shines and for representing skin tones.

REMEMEBER...

- How to arrange your colors on the palette is explained on pages 10 and 11.
- How to mix colors is explained on pages 10 and 11.
- There are different kinds of mixtures. Examples of these are given on pages 14 and 15.

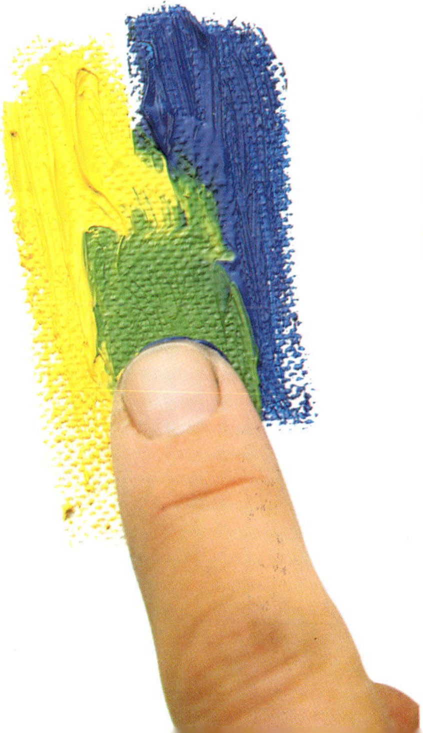

Previously painted colors can be blended on the canvas with a finger, provided that they are still wet.

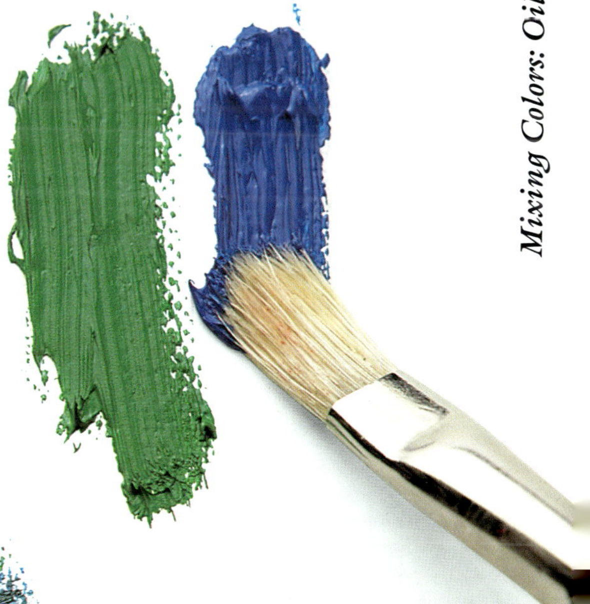

Using a paintbrush, two colors are painted next to each other.

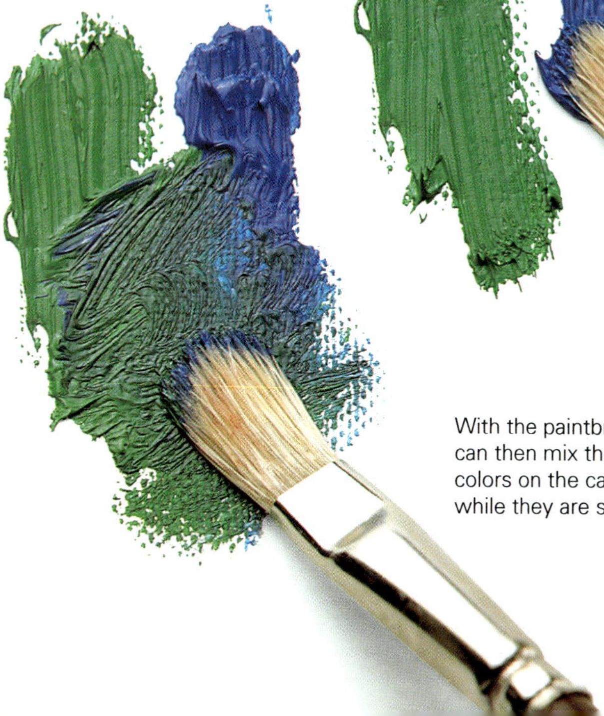

With the paintbrush you can then mix the two colors on the canvas while they are still wet.

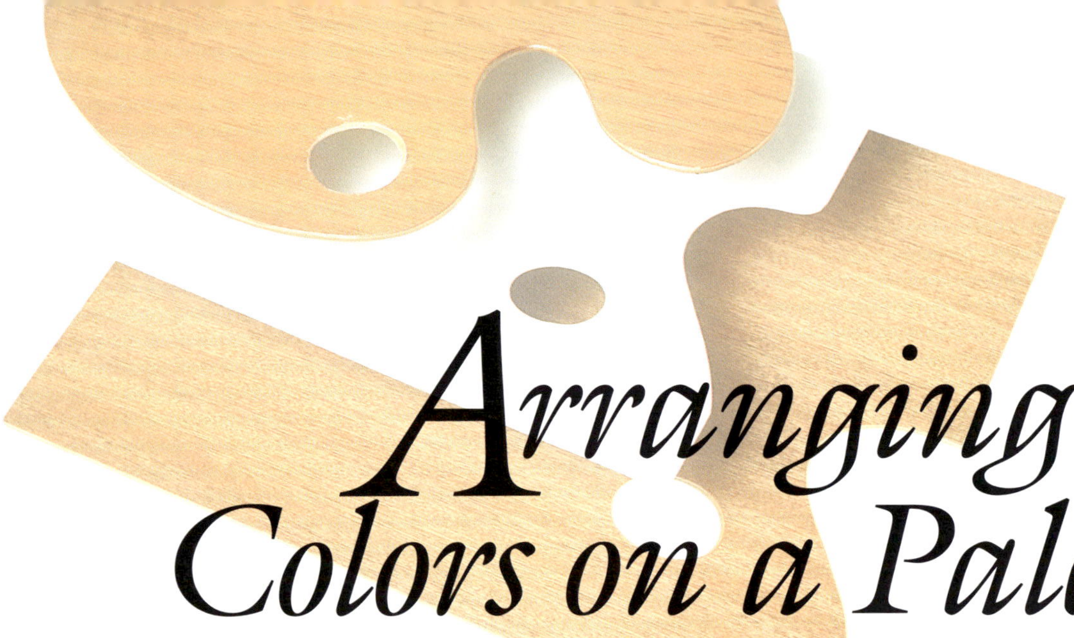

Arranging Colors on a Palette

To mix oil paints, first you have to lay out your colors. Unscrew the cap and squeeze a quantity of paint from each tube onto the palette. Arranging your colors in order will make for quick visual reference as you paint.

Systems for Arranging Colors on the Palette

With each mixing operation you must be able to easily locate the colors you are going to use. If a logical system isn't followed, mixing would be slow and confusing and would likely limit the quality of the end result.

A possible arrangement of colors on a rectangular palette.

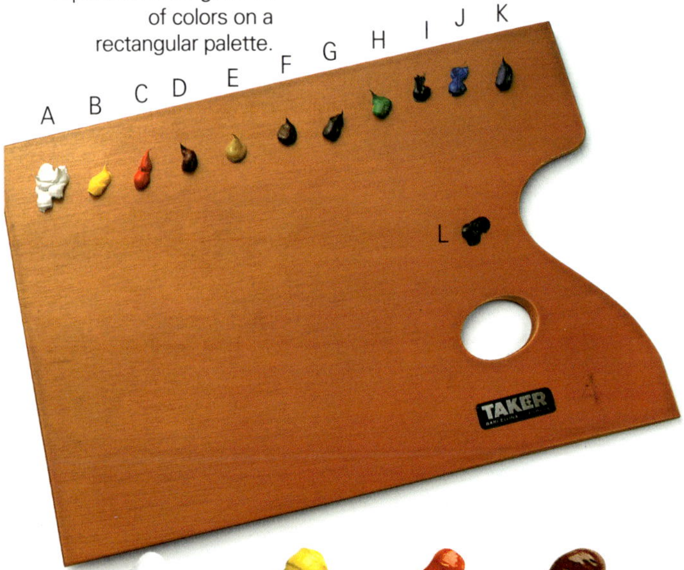

Warm Colors and Cool Colors

One system for arranging the colors on the palette consists of separating the cool colors (blues and greens) from the warm colors (yellows, reds, and earth colors). The cool and warm colors can be further classified according to their intensity. There are several possible correct distributions, which are adaptable to the painter's preferences and the shape of the palette. Palettes can be made of wood, plastic, or disposable sheets of paper. You can even improvise with a ceramic plate. Rectangular palettes are shaped to fit into paintboxes. There are also oval palettes.

Horizontal Arrangement

The colors are arranged in a horizontal line along the top of the palette. They have been distributed from warm to cool according to intensity and color group. Here, the earth colors are grouped together. Another, equally valid option would be to arrange them only in their color groups, integrating the earth tones by color instead.

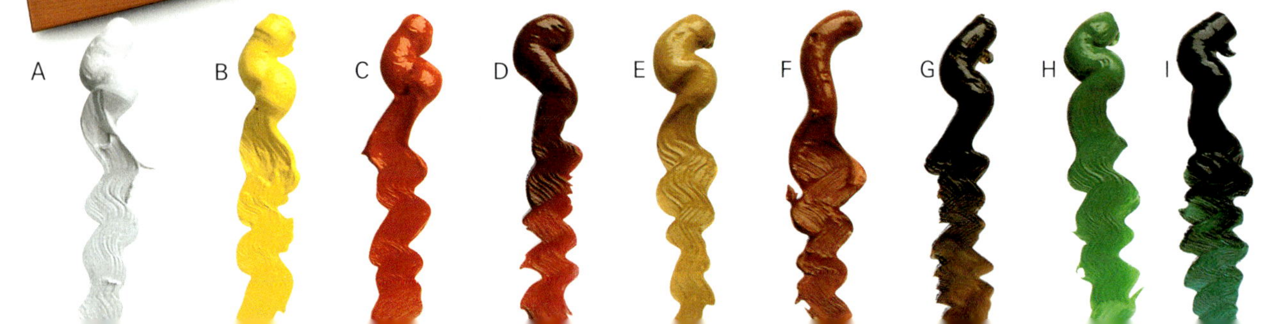

Horizontal and Vertical Arrangement

In this arrangement the difference between warm and cool colors can be clearly seen.

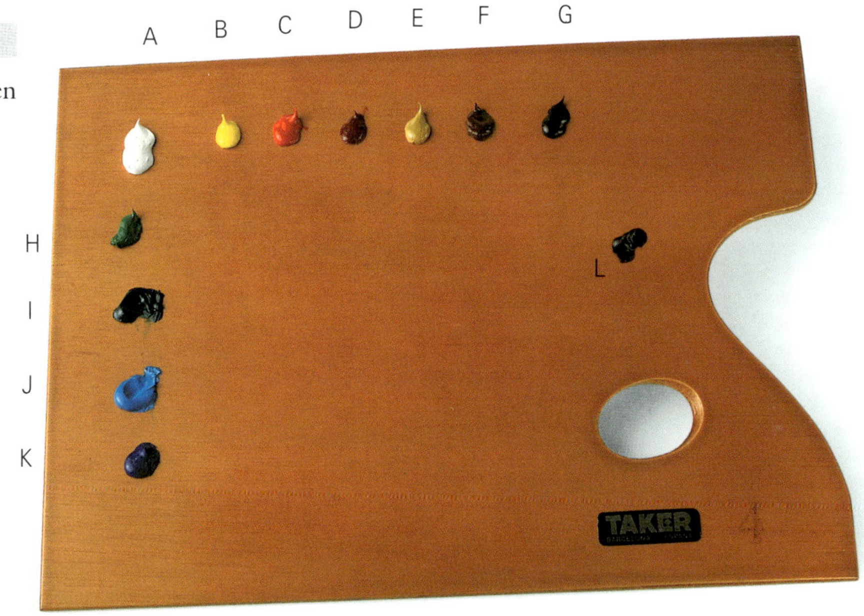

Another way of arranging colors on a rectangular palette.

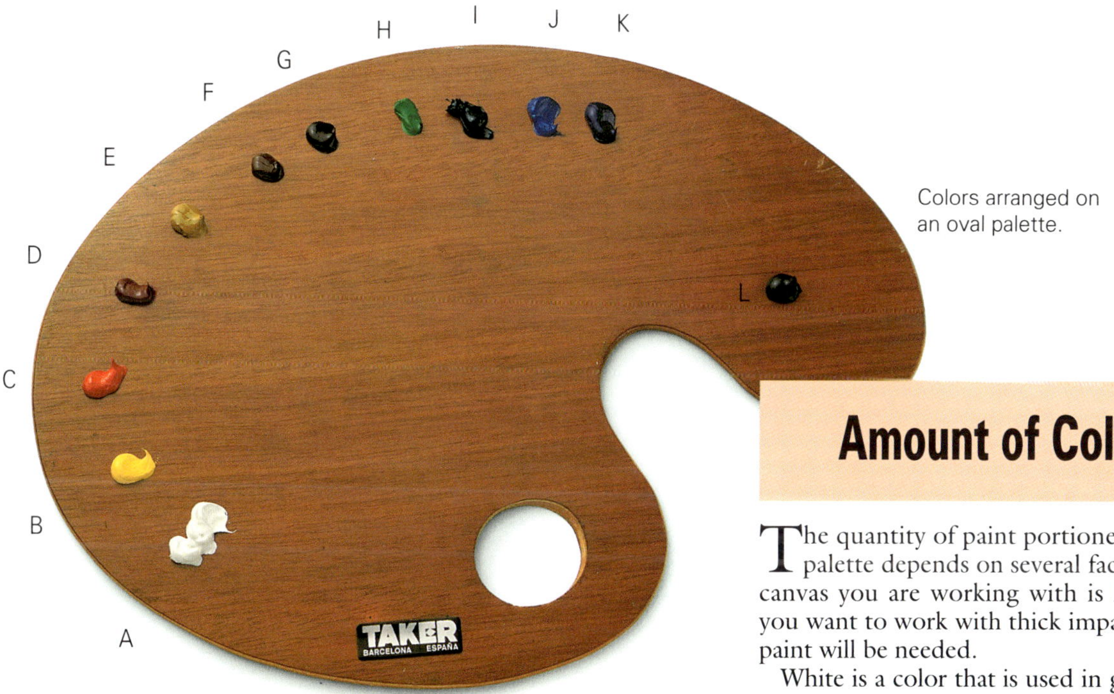

Colors arranged on an oval palette.

Arrangement on an Oval Palette

This is, in fact, the same as the horizontal arrangement on a rectangular palette, but adapted to the curve of the oval.

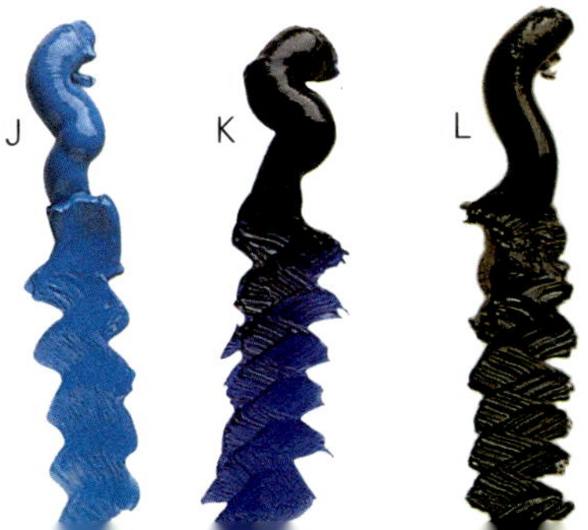

A. White; **B.** Cadmium Yellow; **C.** Vermilion; **D.** Crimson; **E.** Ochre; **F.** Burnt Sienna; **G.** Burnt Umber; **H.** Permanent Green Light; **I.** Chromium Oxide Green; **J.** Winsor Blue; **K.** Ultramarine; **L.** Black.

Amount of Color

The quantity of paint portioned onto the palette depends on several factors. If the canvas you are working with is large, or if you want to work with thick impastos, more paint will be needed.

White is a color that is used in great quantity, so it is best to start out with a bigger portion of white paint than of others. It is advisable to place black, and even umber, a little further away from the rest of the colors.

REMEMBER...

- An orderly palette arrangement of color portions is essential. Experiment, then choose one that suits your mixing best.
- The amount of paint you use depends on the kind of work you are going to do.

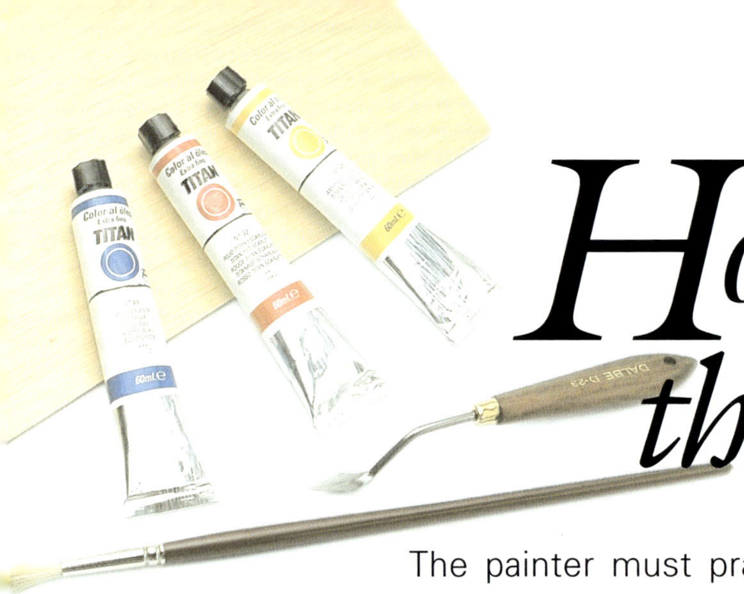

How to Mix the Paint

The painter must practice, above all on the palette, mixing colors with a palette knife or with a paintbrush. For each new mixture, you have to look for a new area on the palette and work with a clean palette knife or paintbrush.

A Mixture of Two Colors

The simplest of mixtures is one made from just two colors. Once they have been chosen, a quantity of each color is separated from its location on the palette and placed on a clean area, laying them side by side. Mix the paints in the space between them. Again, the two most usual tools for mixing are the palette knife and the paintbrush. It is common practice to lay down the paints with the palette knife, then mix them with a clean paintbrush.

Adjusting the Mixture

As you begin to mix, observe the color that results. Perhaps it is not the shade you are trying for. In order to adjust the mixture add a little more of one of the colors, the

1

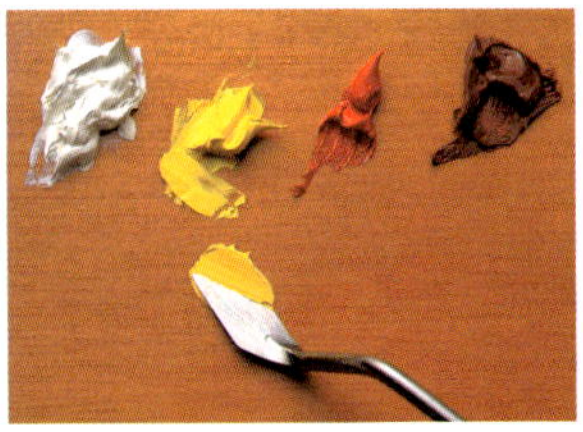

1. Pick up a quantity of yellow paint with the palette knife and place it on a clean area of the palette.

2

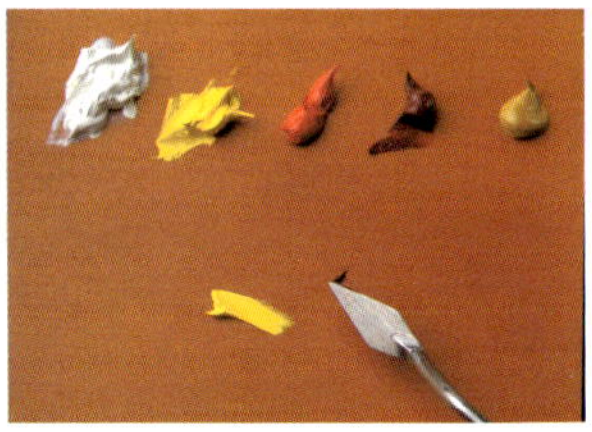

2. Do the same with Burnt Sienna. Press the knife down on the palette in order to deposit all of its paint.

3

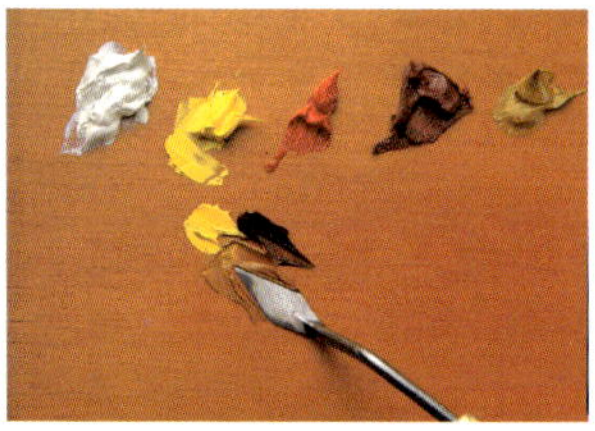

3. Mix both colors with the palette knife. A part of each color contributes to this first mix. Observe the resulting mixed color.

4

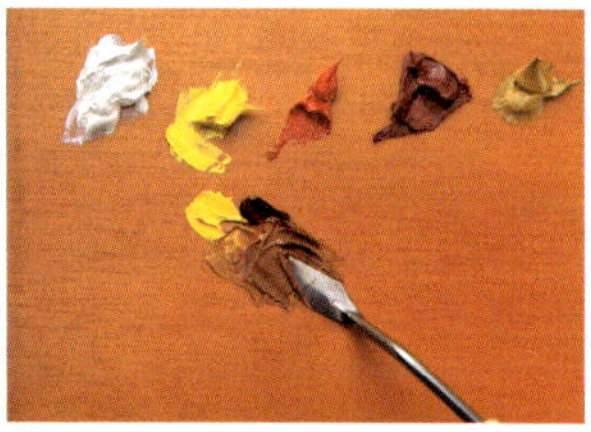

4. As we are looking for a darker color, add a little more sienna to the mixture. Check the difference in color between 3 and 4.

1

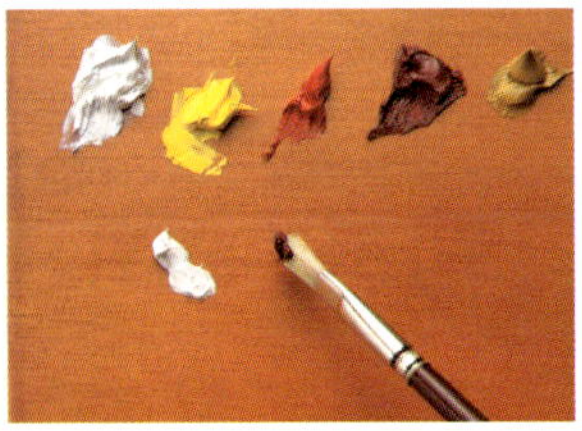

1. Separate a little crimson with a paintbrush. Notice that a clean paintbrush is used. Using a paintbrush that isn't clean would taint the crimson.

2

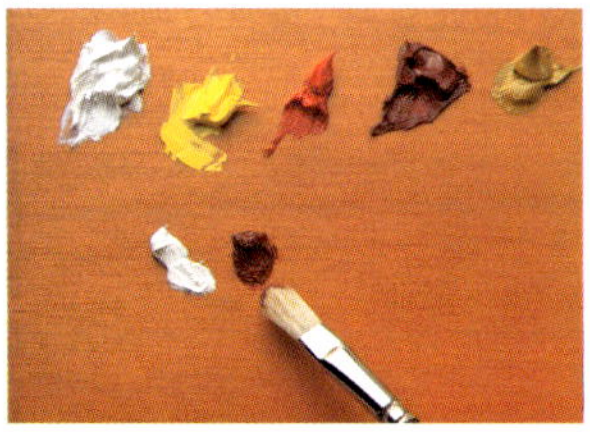

2. Deposit a quantity of crimson close to the white. It is important to leave as much paint as possible from the brush on the palette.

3

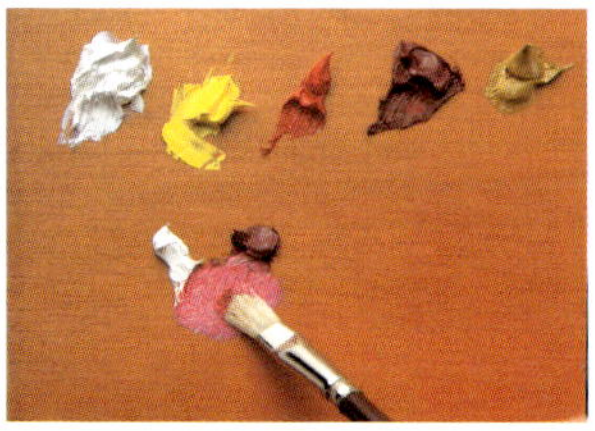

3. Mix the crimson and the white with your paintbrush. Note the color obtained. It is a lighter tone than the one we are looking for. The mixture will have to be adjusted.

4

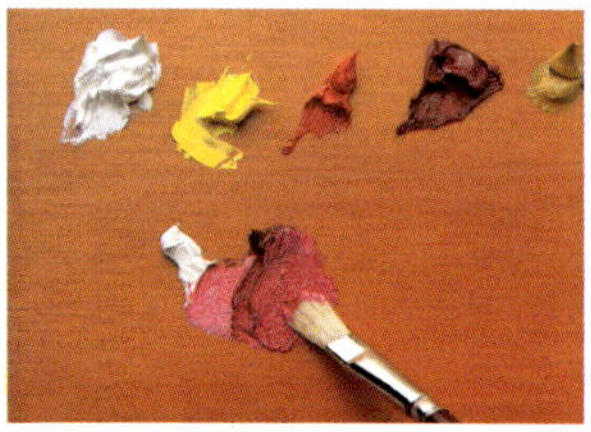

4. Using the paintbrush, brush more crimson into the mixing zone. Now the mixture is adjusted. Compare the result with the color obtained in 3.

one that seems most suited to obtaining the right shade, using the palette knife or the paintbrush. Look at the examples on the previous page.

A Mixture of Several Colors

Mixing gets complicated when three or more colors are used. Suppose you want to achieve a skin tone like the one shown. Begin with portions of the predominant colors in the mixture, a large amount of white, with yellow and vermilion in lesser quantities.

By mixing yellow and vermilion you obtain orange. Then, by mixing the orange and white you will obtain a clean shiny skin tone. To match the color in the example, add a little ochre. By adjusting these three colors, you will eventually obtain a flesh tone very similar to the one shown.

Example of the color we wish to obtain

How to Plan a Mixture

Basically, when creating a mixture two problems have to be solved. First, which colors are needed? And second, in what quantities? As a first example, on this page we are trying to obtain a flesh tone by mixing several colors. From page 18 onward, you will find the theories that will enable you to work out how to create a mixture in a very simple way.

1

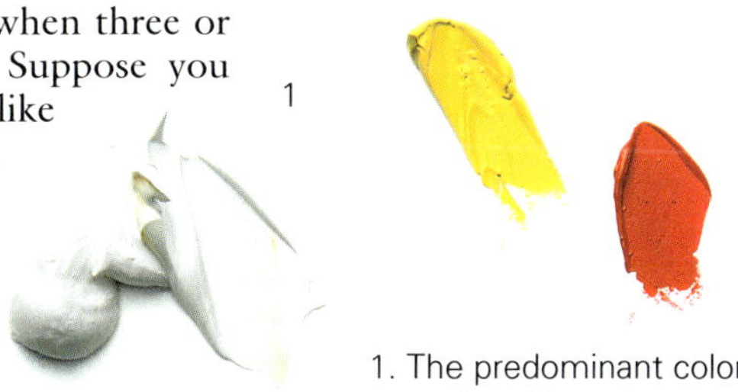

1. The predominant colors are placed in a clean area on the palette.

2

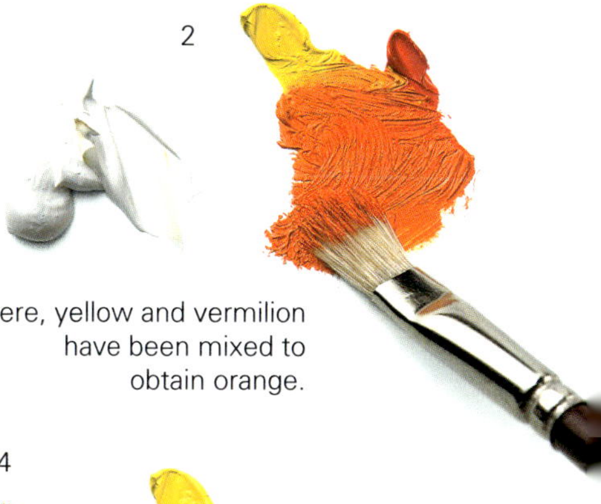

2. Here, yellow and vermilion have been mixed to obtain orange.

3

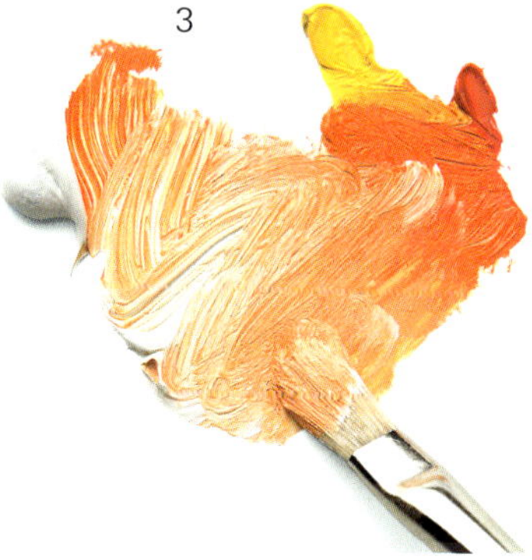

3. The next step is to mix a lot of white into the orange. Note how the resulting mixture resembles the example.

4

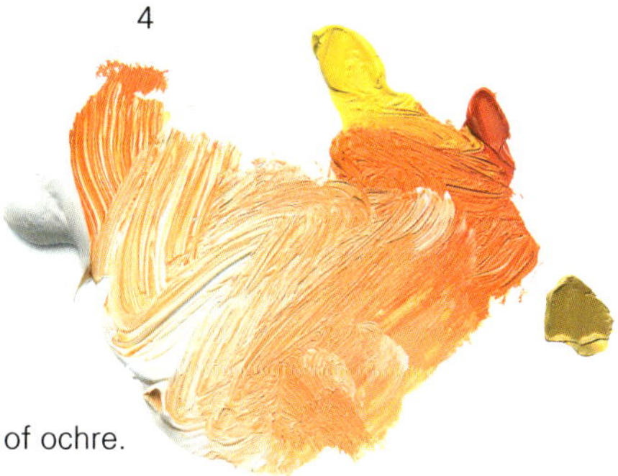

4. Take up a small amount of ochre.

5

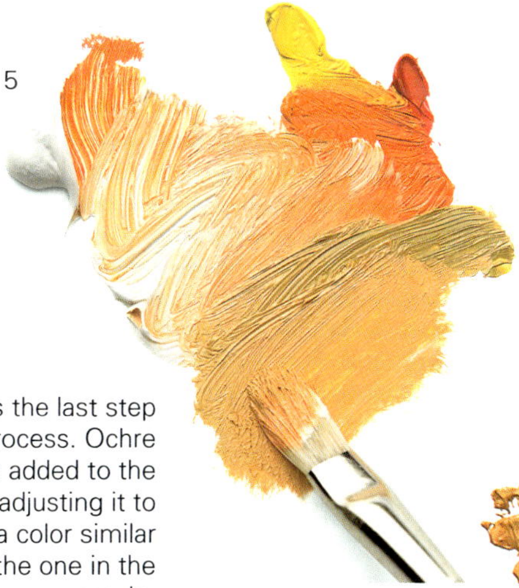

5. This is the last step in the process. Ochre is added to the mixture, adjusting it to achieve a color similar to the one in the example.

6

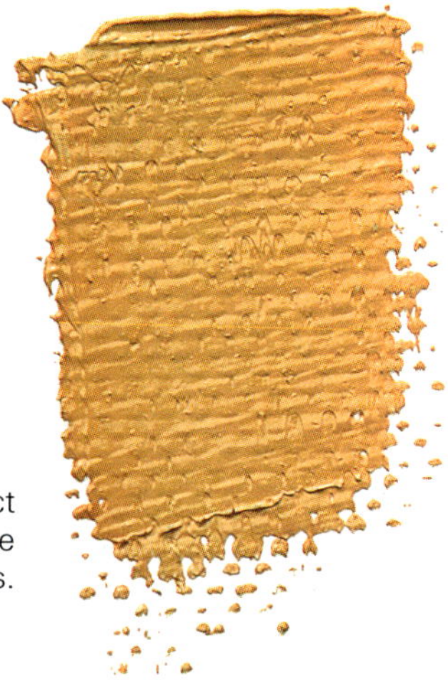

6. Finally, observe the effect of applying this mixture onto canvas.

REMEMBER...

- The palette knife and the paintbrush are the tools we use to mix oil paints.
- In order to create a mixture, we have to take up a certain amount of each color and deposit it on a clean area on the palette.
- Mixtures are obtained by adjusting the amounts of each of the colors that make up the mixture. Work is always done by approximation.

Types of Mixtures

Owing to the diversity of oil paints, we can talk about several different ways of mixing the colors. From physical mixtures to optical mixtures, from opaque paint to transparent paint, wet over wet or wet over dry, the aim is always the same: to greatly increase your color spectrum.

Physical Mixtures

Depending on the degree of uniformity present in a color mixture, we can say it is either a physical mixture or an optical mixture. A physical mixture of two wet colors appears uniform as the colors are blended thoroughly with the palette knife on the palette. Look at the example in figure 1.

Now let's go on to working with impastos, using a large amount of paint and working it in thick applications so that it stands out from the canvas. Although the paint takes some time to dry, the results are very attractive. In figure 2 the mixing is not thorough and swirls of each of the colors can be clearly distinguished. But the visual effect is nevertheless of one color that, instead of being mixed on the palette, is mixed in the retina of the eye.

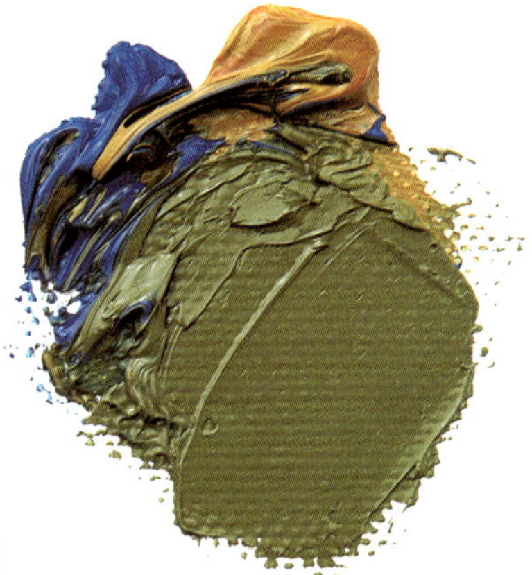

1. A very uniform physical mixture.

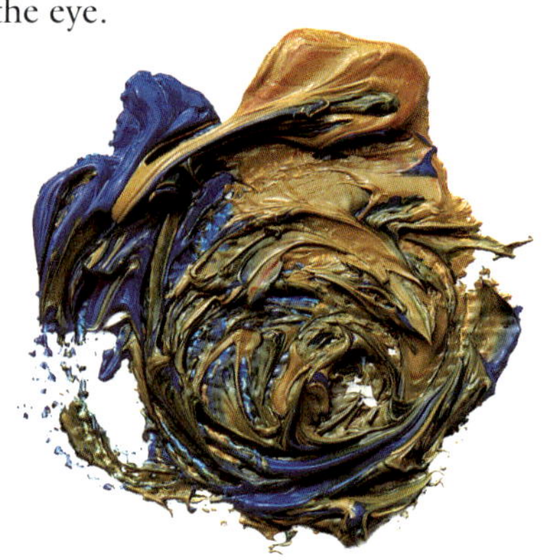

2. A barely blended mixture of two wet colors.

REMEMBER...

- In oil painting, mixtures of colors can be achieved by several different methods.
- Colors can be mixed physically, wet on wet, on the palette, or directly on the canvas.
- Mixtures can be obtained by glazing wet over dry.
- Frottage or glazing in thin layers of opaque paint is yet another resource for toning a color.

Optical Mixtures

There are many ways of producing optical mixtures, those that are produced in the retina from a certain distance. The impressionists were very interested in this phenomenon. Look at some simple examples. Brushstrokes can be painted side by side, or the technique of pointillism, small points of color, can also be used. Furthermore, by playing with the contrasts between tones and colors, optical mixtures can be very rich.

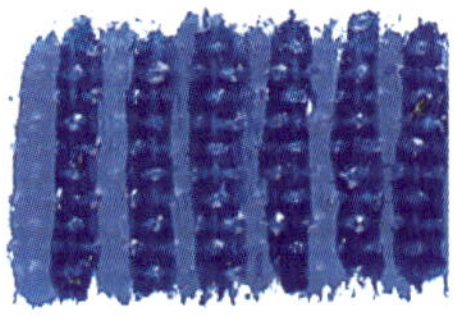

3. Side-by-side brushstrokes of Winsor Blue and ultramarine. From the right distance, the effect is of an intermediate blue.

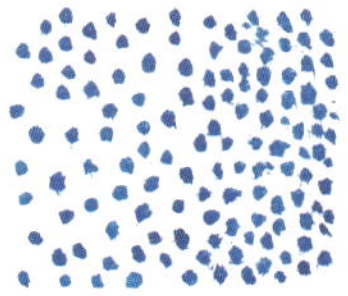

4. Here we have pointillism in blue on a white background.

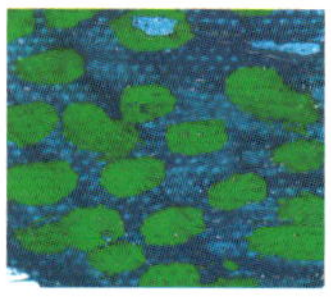

5. On the other hand, the contrast obtained with medium green on a blue background produces quite a different effect.

Glazes

One way of working in oils is by diluting the density of the paint with linseed oil or turpentine. A very transparent color is obtained. With oil, the paint shines, while with turpentine, the finish is dulled.

When a transparent color is applied over another color, which has already dried, a glaze will be achieved. As can be seen in the illustration, glazing in this way results in a color effect quite different from that which would be achieved through blending two wet colors.

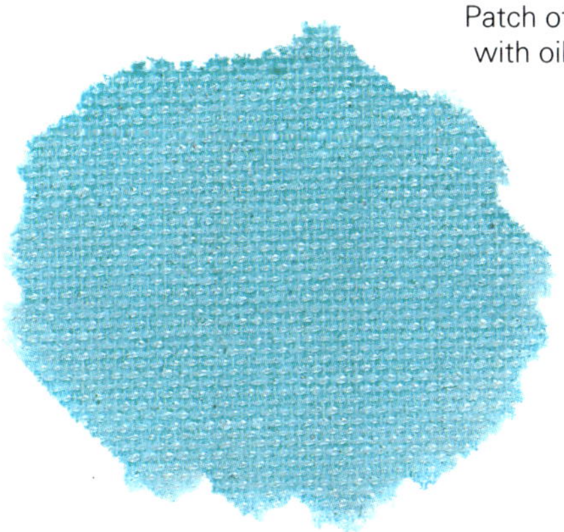

Patch of Winsor Blue diluted with oil and turpentine. This is a transparency.

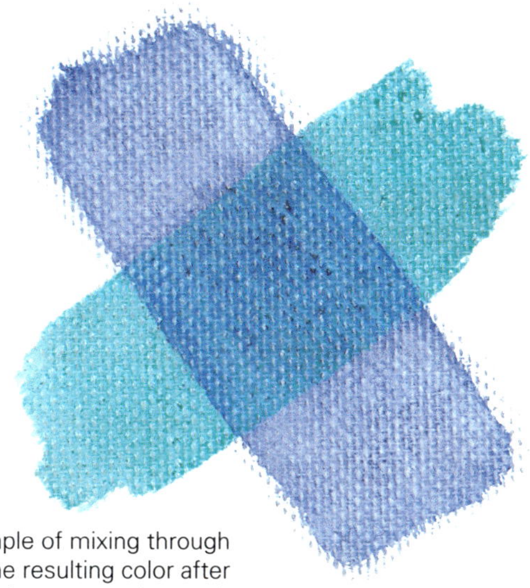

An example of mixing through transparency. The resulting color after applying a glaze over a dry patch of Winsor Blue is different from a mix of wet paints.

Another Method

By means of scrubbing, or frottage, special effects can be obtained. Let's see how. With a clean, dry paintbrush, take up a small amount of paint and scrub over a dry area of the canvas that has been previously painted with another color. In effect we are rubbing an opaque color, although in a small amount, over dry paint. We have carried out two frottages, one with orange and the other with Winsor Blue lightened with white. Observe the results obtained. Oil paints permit an infinite number of possibilities.

Different Effects to Achieve the Same End

Whatever method we use, the result remains the same: to mix colors. The plastic qualities are evidently different. The results of the mixture may be dull or glossy, opaque or transparent. This is the secret of the universality of oil paint, its infinite possibilities for achieving shades and color tones.

Two frottages over a dry ultramarine background. One with orange, mixed from vermilion and yellow. The other with Winsor Blue lightened with white.

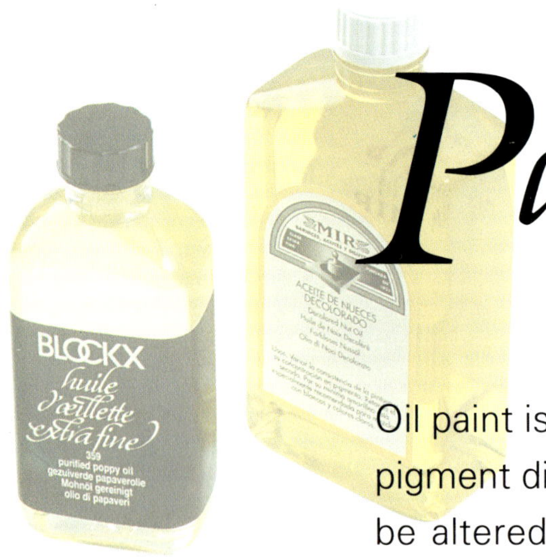

Paint Density

Oil paint is a greasy painting medium that is made up from a color pigment dissolved in oil and turpentine. The density can, therefore, be altered by adding more oil and turpentine. The following will clarify this process.

Mixing on the Palette

When you begin to mix your colors on the palette, use the paints just as they come out of the tube. The density of manufactured oil paints is intended to ease the job of mixing.

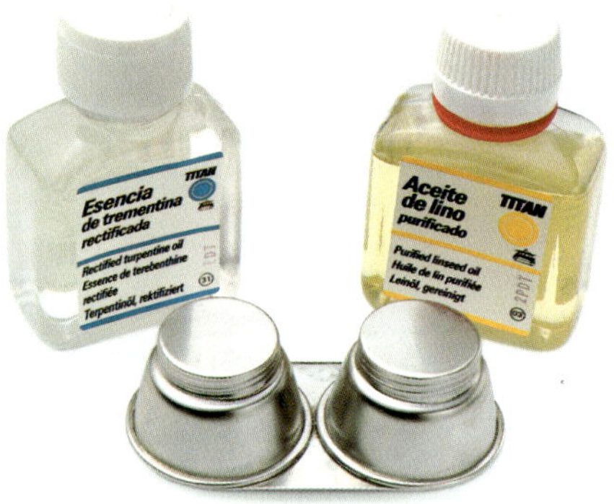

Rectified spirit of turpentine, linseed oil, and palette cups.

Mixing on the Canvas

When applying oil paints to a fresh canvas, however, the paint should be diluted. To do this you will need a jar or palette cups in which to prepare a solution of linseed oil (60%) and rectified turpentine (40%). Both the palette knife and the paintbrush can be used to dilute the paint, by dipping either tool into the oil and turpentine, then adding quantities of the mixture to the paint.

Mixtures of paints are opaque unless they are diluted. On the other hand, mixtures that have been thinned, by adding an oil and spirit of turpentine solution to them, appear more transparent.

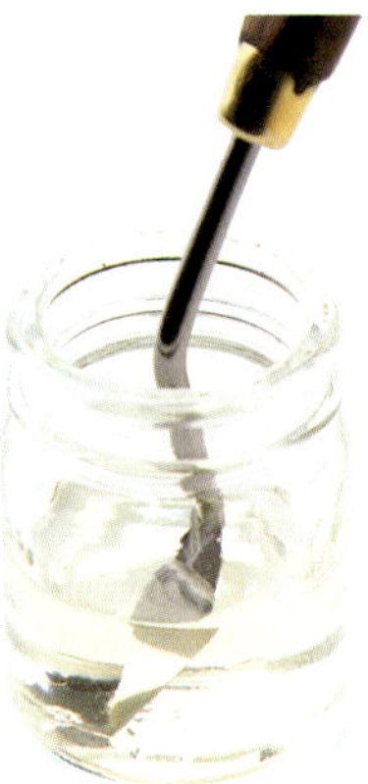

On taking the palette knife out of the solution, an amount of thinner is carried with it.

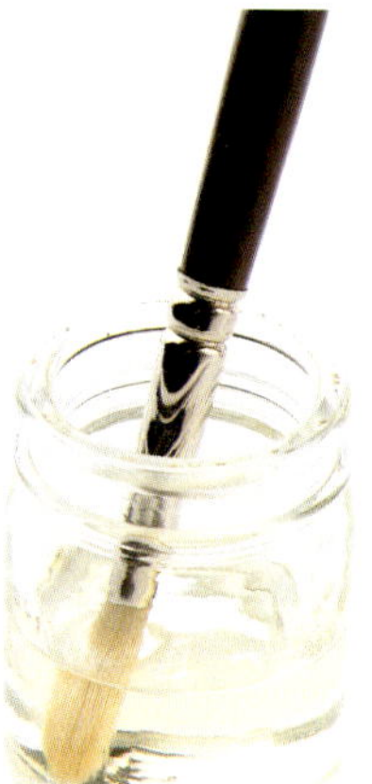

A paintbrush will also carry a quantity of thinner.

An example on canvas of an opaque mixture of crimson and Winsor Blue.

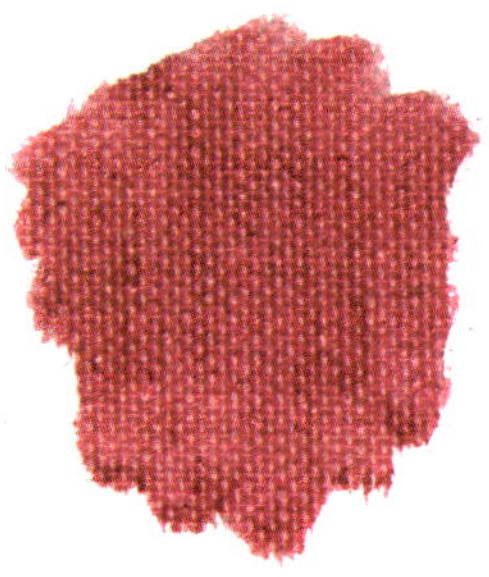

Now the mixture appears transparent after having been diluted with a solution of spirit and oil.

REMEMBER...

- The first patches of color on a clean canvas need a greater amount of thinning solution. This is not the case with successive layers of paint.
- When the part of the palette used for mixing is dirty, it must be thoroughly cleaned using turpentine.

Problems and Solutions

There are a number of problems that crop up when you begin to work with oils. Most of them have simple solutions. Here are some of them.

The thickness of paint straight from the tube may vary from one color to another. The more oil the color contains, the less thinner will need to be added to it.

If a tube has been put away without cleaning it, paint may accumulate around the cap. If this sticks tight, the top should be held close to the flame of a cigarette lighter or match. With heat, the paint will melt and the tube can be opened.

It is recommended that you clean paint tubes before putting them away at the end of a work session. Remove accumulated paint from around the threaded part of the cap with a paper towel. When kept together, closed dirty tubes may contaminate each other. When used again, paint emerging from a tube may be tainted with another color. This simple fact may spoil the result of a mixture.

State of the paint when it comes out of the tube. This may vary according to brands and colors. It depends on the batch.

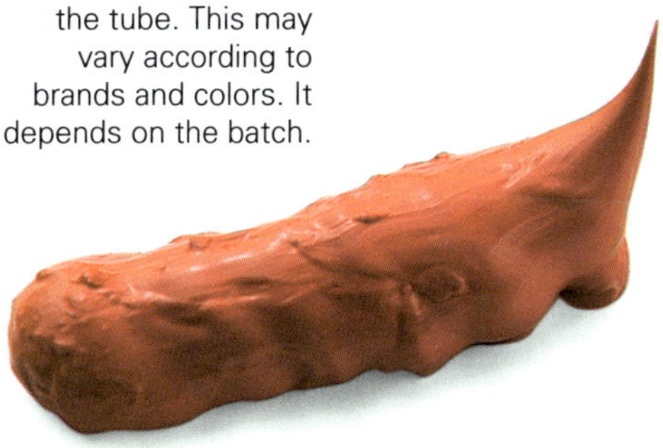

A tube put away while still dirty.

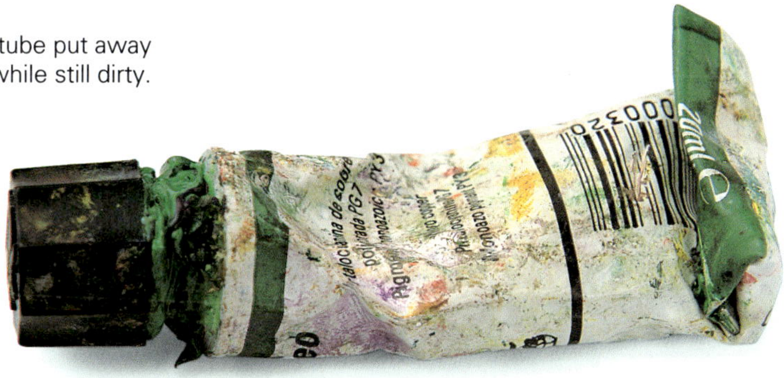

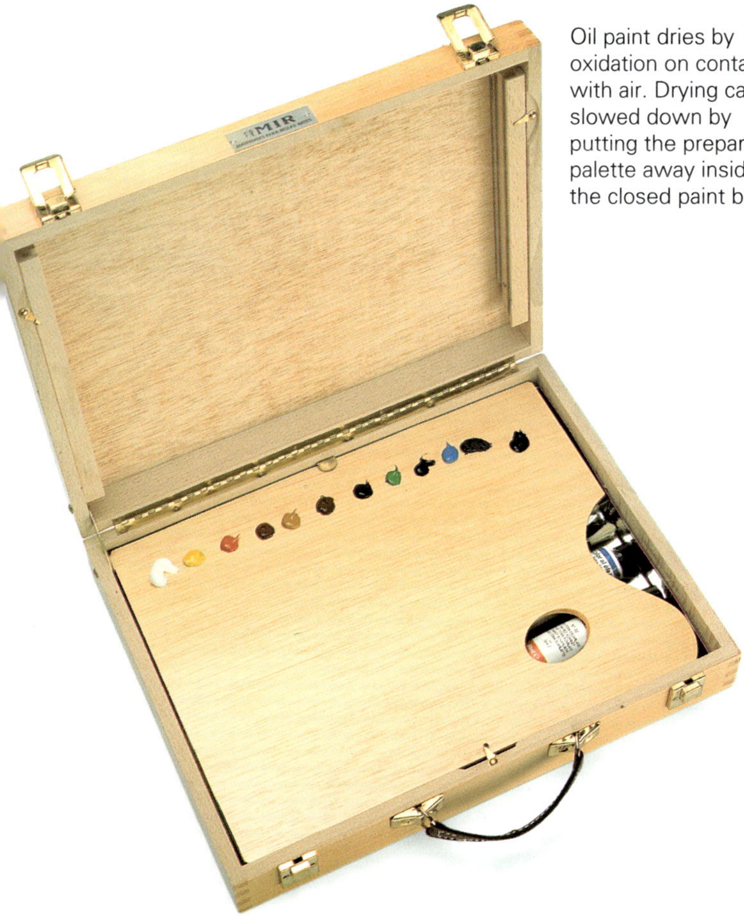

Oil paint dries by oxidation on contact with air. Drying can be slowed down by putting the prepared palette away inside the closed paint box.

A stubborn tube can be opened with the heat from a cigarette lighter or match.

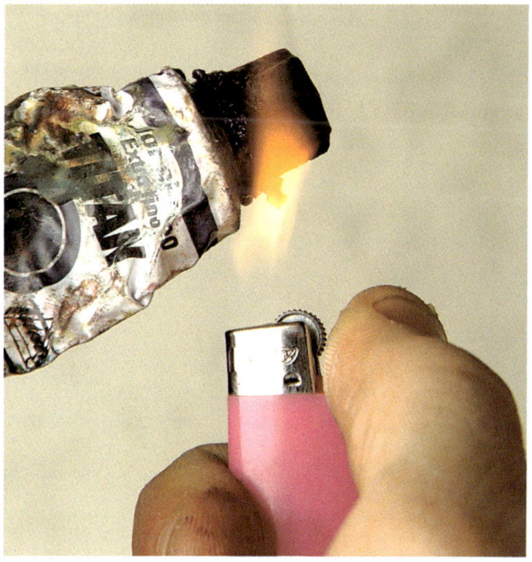

Paint Dries on the Palette

As oil paint dries on contact with air, some rules should be followed. The palette's mixing area should be thoroughly cleaned. The palette should be placed in the drawer of the paint box, which is then closed to keep the unused portions of paint moist and ready for their next use.

Primary and Secondary Colors

There are some basic principles for mixing oil paints. All colors are mixed from three basic, or primary, colors: red, yellow, and blue. Red and yellow mix orange; blue and yellow mix green; blue and red mix violet, which are the secondary colors. In physical fact, however, only light is pure enough to result in pure colors when mixed. In paint, different pigments have their own physical and chemical properties.*

*There are many systems of color mixing, many terminologies that may overlap and even at times seem to contradict. The color mixing system presented here applies the terms "secondary" and "tertiary" to the colors that will result when using this particular palette of pigments.

Three Primary Colors: Yellow, Crimson, and Blue

On our suggested palette, the basic or primary colors are Light Cadmium Yellow, Alizarin Crimson, and Winsor Blue. Starting out from these primary colors, and by mixing each pair, our secondary and tertiary colors are formed. See pages 19, 20, and 21.

Yellow

Of the three basic colors, yellow is the lightest and brightest. Mixing yellow with one of the other primary colors will darken it.

Light Cadmium Yellow

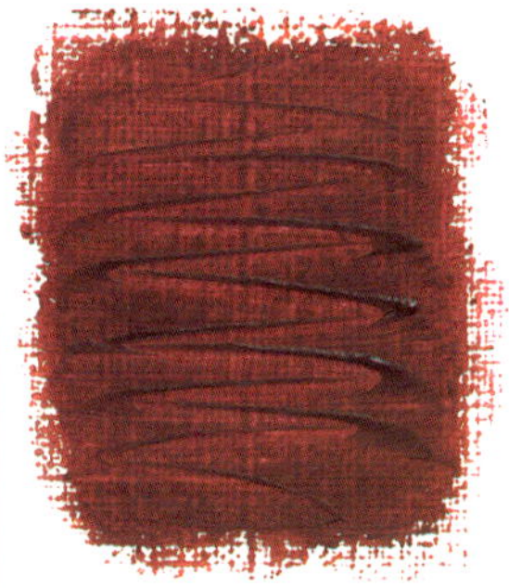

Crimson

Alizarin Crimson is the nearest oil color to magenta, a tincture pigment that mixes very pure violets. Yellow and crimson are warm colors, as opposed to blue, which is a cool color.

Alizarin Crimson

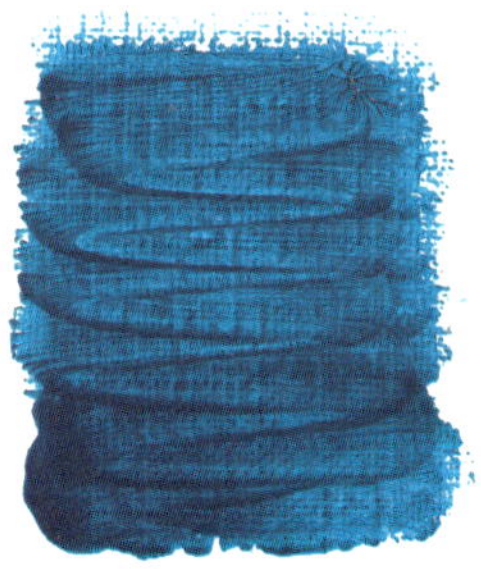

Winsor Blue

This blue is a warmer blue than ultramarine, which is cooler.

Winsor Blue

REMEMBER...

- The three basic, or primary, colors are fundamental. By mixing them, a painter can obtain any other color he or she may need.
- When two primary colors are mixed, clean colors are obtained.
- By mixing three primary colors, gray or muddy colors are obtained.
- The three basic colors mixed in equal parts form a deep gray—almost black, the absence of color.

Secondary Colors: Red, Green, and Purple-Blue

Theoretically, a secondary color is obtained by mixing two primary colors in equal parts. There will be, therefore, three secondary colors. By mixing yellow and crimson in equal parts, red is obtained. By mixing yellow and Winsor Blue in equal parts, green is obtained. By mixing Winsor Blue and crimson in equal parts, the secondary purple-blue is obtained.

Practice

Right from the first experience with the palette, you will realize that it is not easy to take up equal measures of paint. Whether with the palette knife or with the paintbrush, measurement is always by guesswork. Thus, the first thing that should be understood is that a painter hardly ever obtains a color right away but works toward it by adjusting the quantities of colors that he or she is mixing. Observe how the red, green, and deep blue secondary colors are achieved.

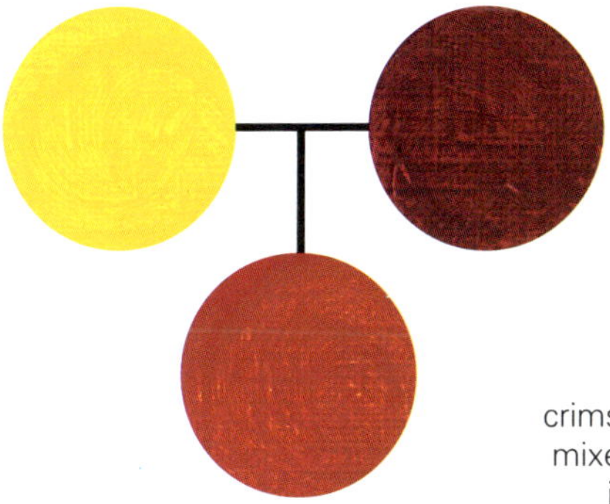

Red

In theory, the secondary red color is obtained by mixing yellow and crimson in equal parts.

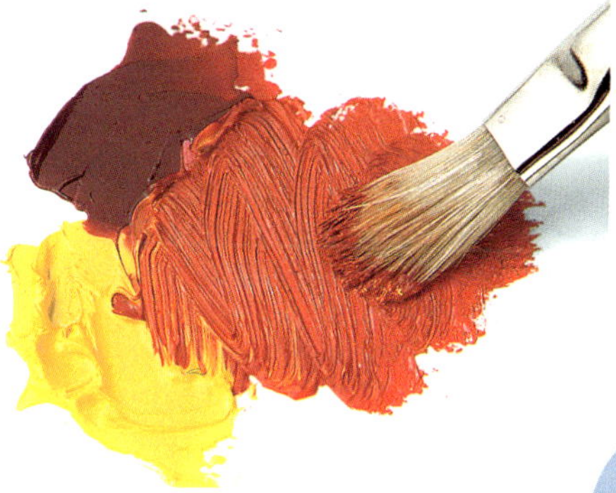

In practice, equal parts of the two colors, crimson and yellow, are taken up. They are then mixed in the middle of the palette and the color is adjusted until it takes on the desired hue.

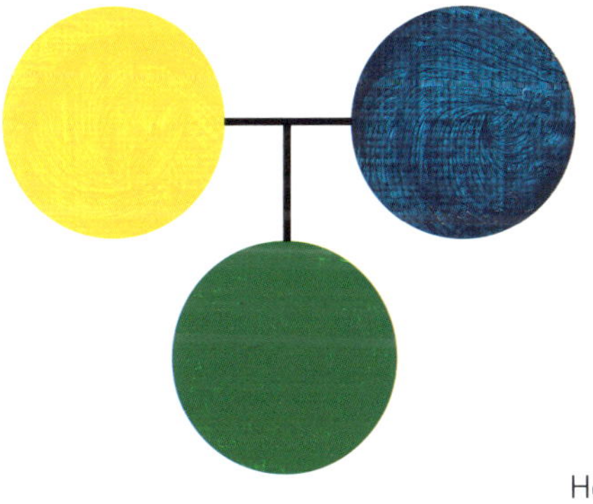

Green

The secondary green is created using yellow and Winsor Blue.

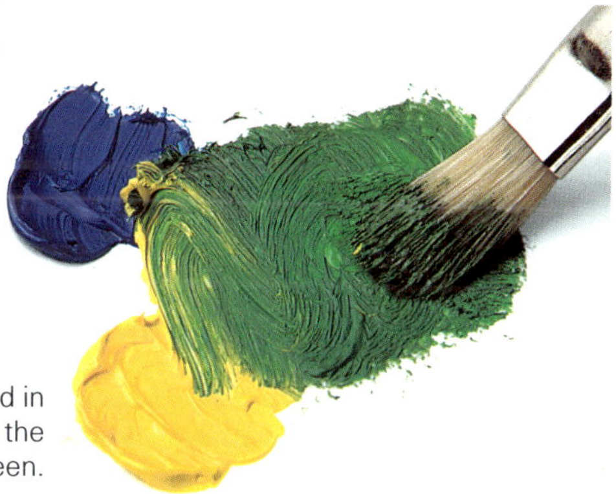

Here, yellow and Winsor Blue are separated in similar quantities. They are blended to obtain the secondary green.

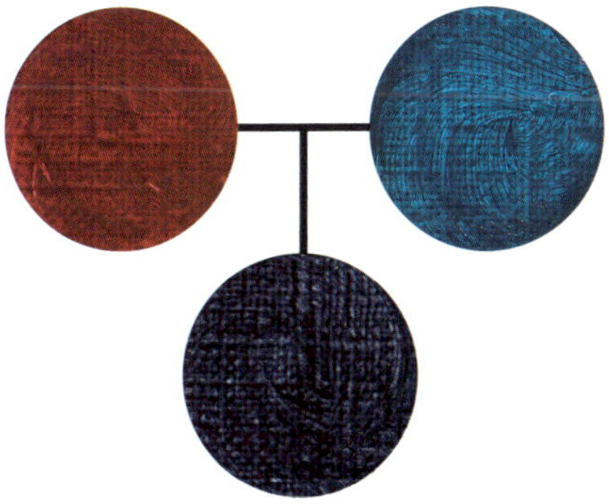

Purple-Blue

Equal parts of the primary colors, Winsor Blue and crimson, make up the secondary color, purple-blue.

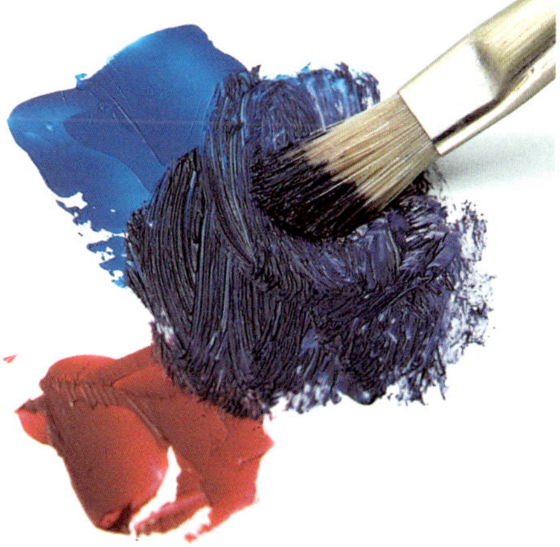

Starting from the mixture of crimson and Winsor Blue, the color is adjusted to obtain the deep secondary blue.

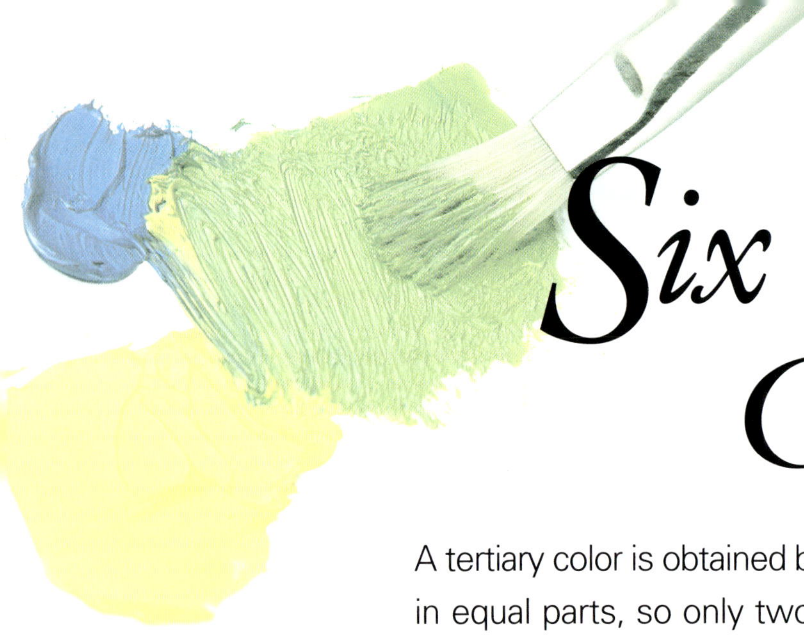

Six Tertiary Colors

A tertiary color is obtained by mixing a secondary and a primary color in equal parts, so only two primary colors are involved at any one time. There are six tertiary colors in the system presented here: orange, crimson-red, violet, violet-blue, blue-green, and yellow-green.

REMEMBER...

- The three secondary colors and the six tertiary colors are colors of reference.
- Secondary and tertiary colors are all clean colors. To obtain them, only two primary colors are employed at a time.

Theory

A tertiary color is obtained by mixing a secondary and a primary color in equal parts, where a total of only two primary colors are present. A tertiary color is, therefore the result of mixing two primary colors, as when mixing a secondary color, but with a different proportion as regards the amount. In theory, two primary colors are mixed together in equal parts to obtain a secondary color. In turn, the secondary color is mixed in equal parts with one of the two primary colors previously mixed. The result is a tertiary color.

Practice

Look at the practical application of the theory. In order to obtain a tertiary color, you have to add more of one primary color than the other. The proportion is 75% to 25%. In practice, a painter takes up two primary colors in differing amounts and simply proceeds to adjust the final mixture until it visually approaches the theoretical tertiary color.

Orange

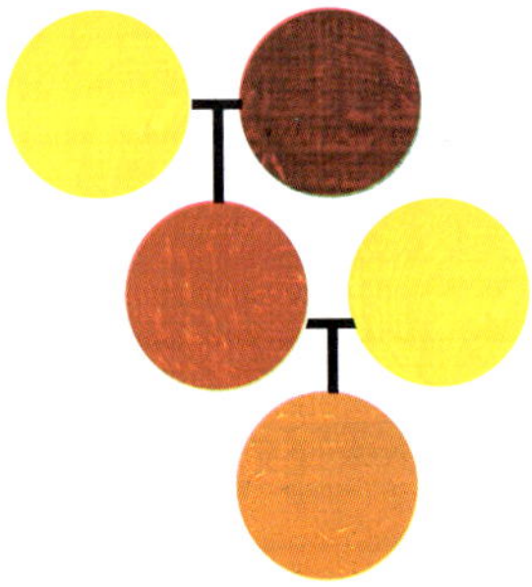

Secondary orange or warm red (obtained by mixing yellow and crimson in equal parts) is mixed in equal parts with yellow. The result is tertiary orange.

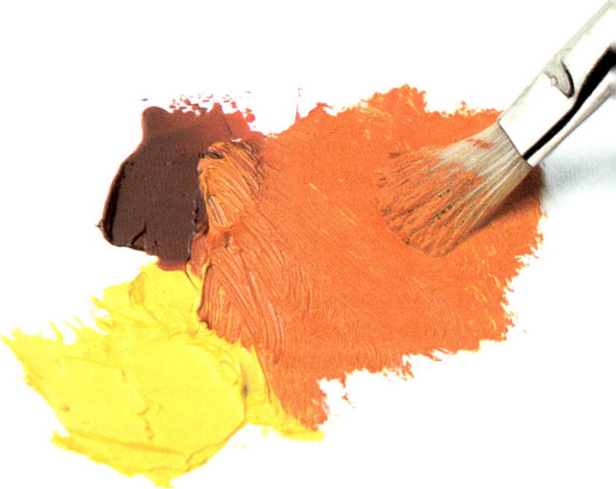

The painter uses the two primary colors needed to obtain tertiary orange. He or she is able to adjust the mixture knowing that there is always a proportion of 75% yellow and 25% crimson.

Crimson-red

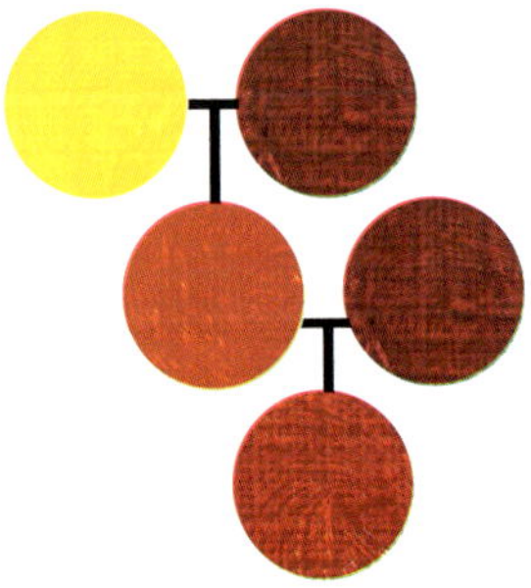

Secondary orange (obtained by mixing yellow and crimson in equal parts) is mixed in equal parts with crimson. The result is tertiary crimson-red.

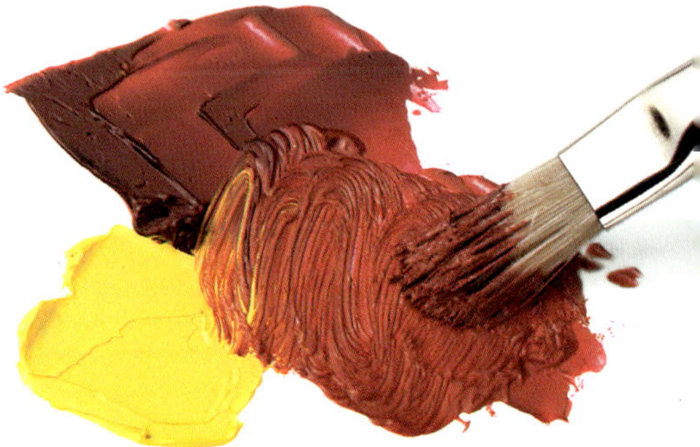

The painter uses the two primary colors needed to obtain tertiary orange. The mixture can then be adjusted knowing that there is always a proportion of 25% yellow and 75% crimson.

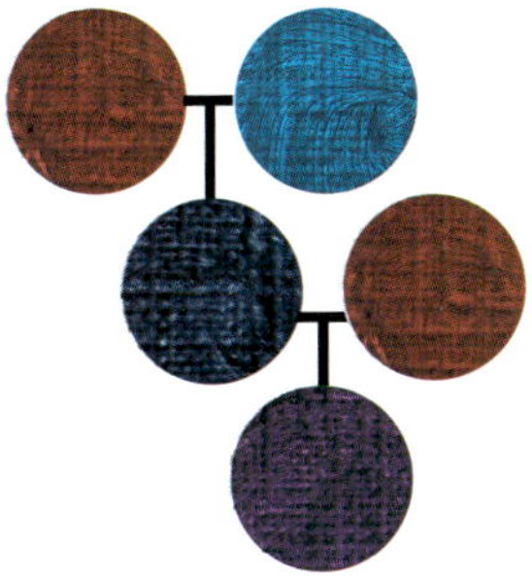

Violet

Secondary blue (obtained by mixing Winsor Blue and crimson in equal parts) is mixed in equal parts with crimson. The result is tertiary violet.

The painter uses the two primary colors needed to obtain tertiary violet. The mixture can then be adjusted with a proportion of 25% Winsor Blue and 75% crimson.

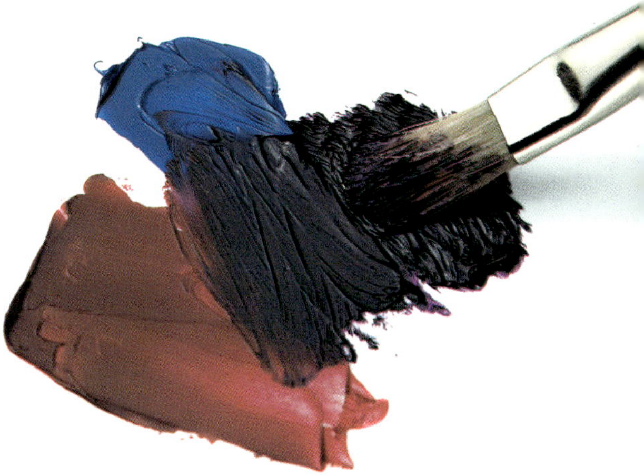

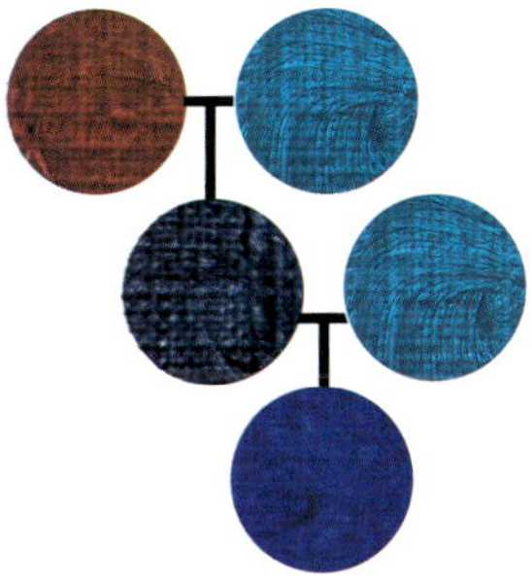

Violet-blue

Secondary blue (obtained by mixing Winsor Blue and crimson in equal parts) is mixed in equal parts with Winsor Blue. The result is tertiary violet-blue.

The painter uses the two primary colors needed to obtain tertiary violet-blue. The mixture can then be adjusted knowing that there is always a proportion of 75% Winsor Blue and 25% crimson.

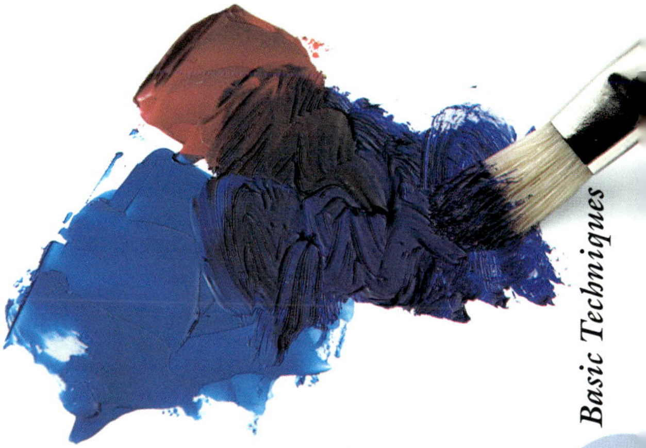

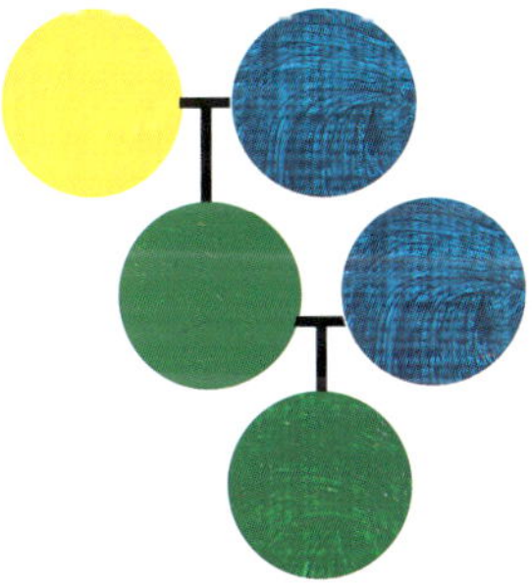

Blue-green

Secondary green (obtained by mixing Winsor Blue and yellow in equal parts) is mixed in equal parts with Winsor Blue. The result is tertiary blue-green.

The painter mixes the two primary colors needed to obtain tertiary blue-green, using a proportion of 75% blue and 25% yellow.

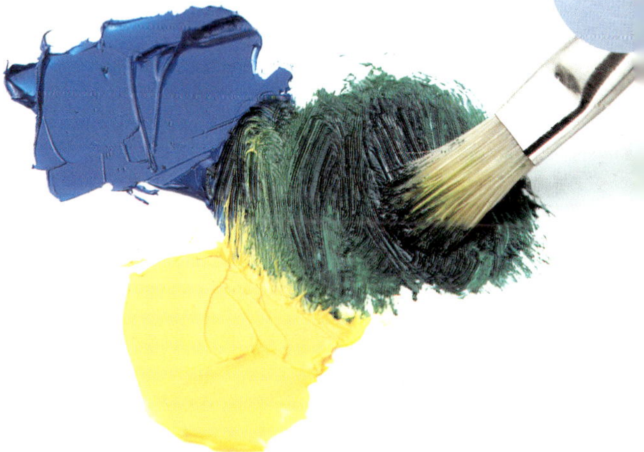

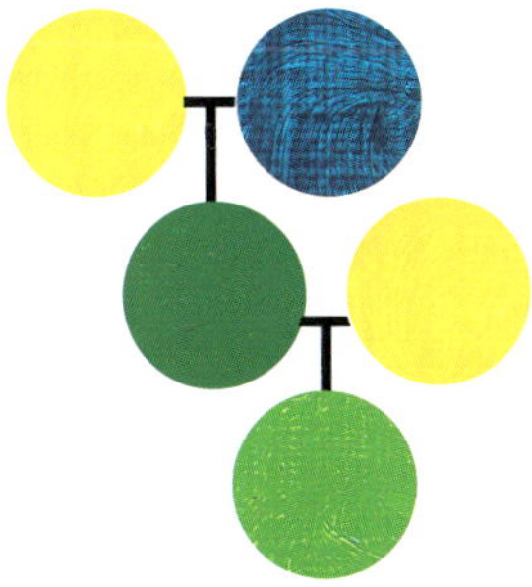

Yellow-green

Secondary green (obtained by mixing Winsor Blue and yellow in equal parts) is mixed in equal parts with yellow. The result is tertiary yellow-green.

The painter uses the two primary colors needed to obtain tertiary yellow-green, then adjusts the mixture using a proportion of 25% blue and 75% yellow.

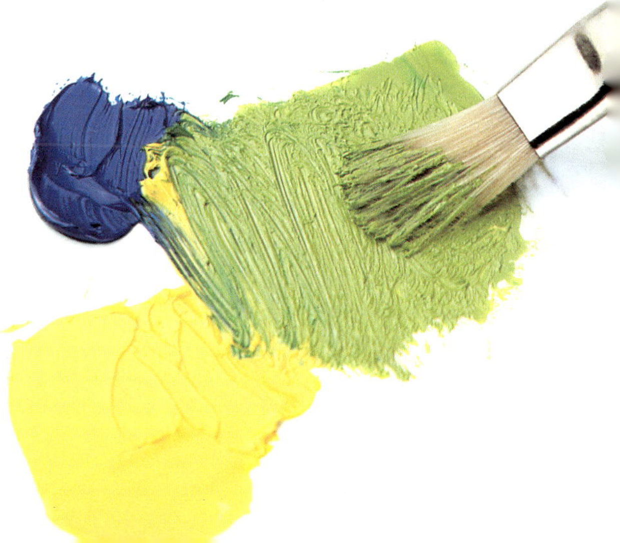

Contrasting Colors

There are colors that, when placed next to each other, produce the maximum possible color contrast. It is important to be familiar with these and their use in painting.

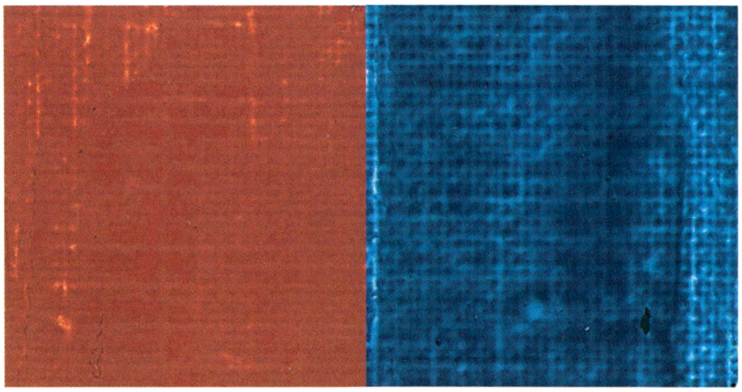

Blue and Warm Red

Winsor Blue creates a strong contrast with secondary orange or warm red.

Remember that secondary orange is obtained by mixing yellow and crimson in equal parts.

The complementary color to secondary orange is the other primary color, Winsor Blue, which does not form part of its composition.

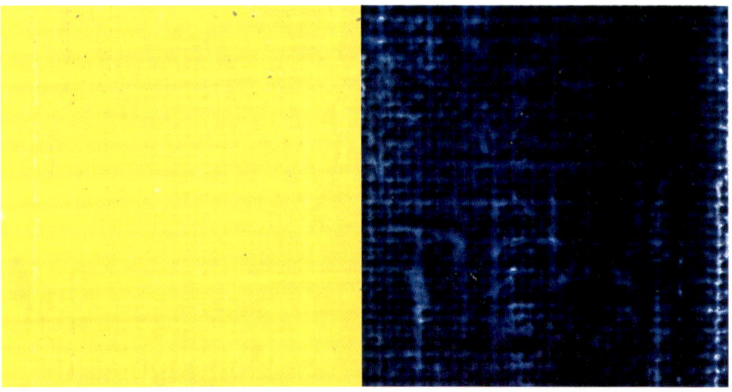

Yellow and Purple-Blue

Yellow contrasts strongly with purple-blue. Secondary purple-blue is the result of mixing Winsor Blue and crimson in equal parts.

The complementary color to purple-blue is yellow, which does not form part of its composition.

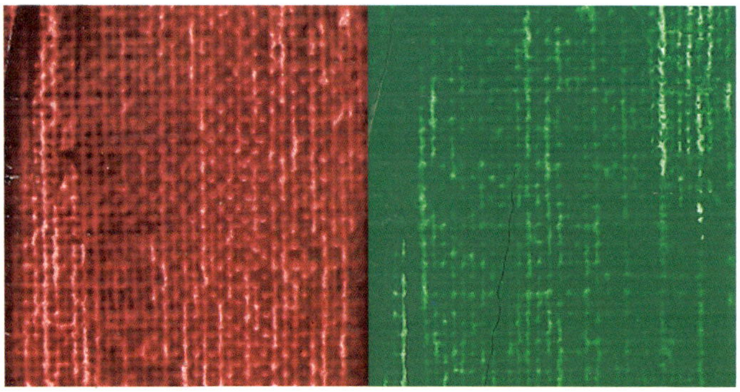

Crimson and Green

Crimson contrasts strongly with green. Green is the secondary color resulting from the mixture of yellow and Winsor Blue in equal parts.

The complementary color to green is crimson, which does not form part of its composition.

Mixtures of Complementary Colors

Red and green, yellow and violet, and orange and blue are the complementary colors. When two pairs are mixed, we are actually mixing the three primary colors together. Remember that when mixed in equal proportions, the result is almost black, as opposed to unequal proportions, which yield gray, muddy-looking colors.

When crimson and secondary green are mixed in equal parts, a very dark color, almost black, is obtained.

If you add a small amount of Winsor Blue to secondary red, a dark purple is obtained, which can be heightened by adding a little white.

REMEMBER...

- The mixing of complementary colors in equal parts produces very gray, almost black, colors.
- Mixtures of complementary colors in unequal quantities, with or without the addition of white, produces broken colors.

Definition of Neutral or Broken Color

A neutral or broken color is obtained by mixing two complementary colors in unequal proportions, with or without the addition of white. To create a neutral color, the contribution of primary colors is very unequal.

With a mixture of yellow and secondary deep blue, in equal parts, a very dark, greenish color is obtained.

From a mixture of secondary red and Winsor Blue, in equal parts, a very dark undefined color is obtained.

Here is another broken color. A lot of yellow has been mixed with a small amount of deep blue. The color obtained is greenish.

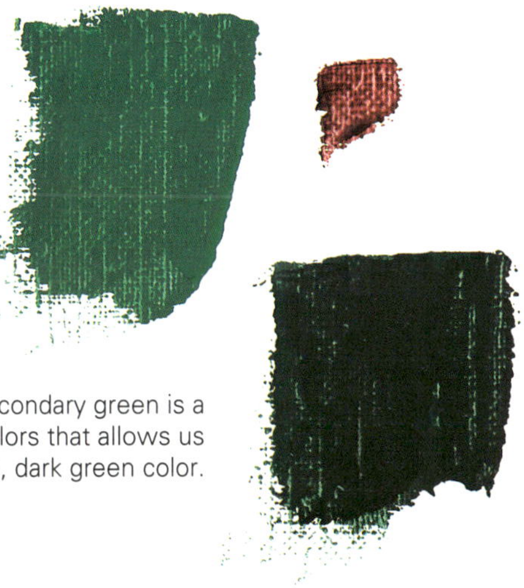

A little crimson and a lot of secondary green is a mixture of complementary colors that allows us to obtain a grayish, dark green color.

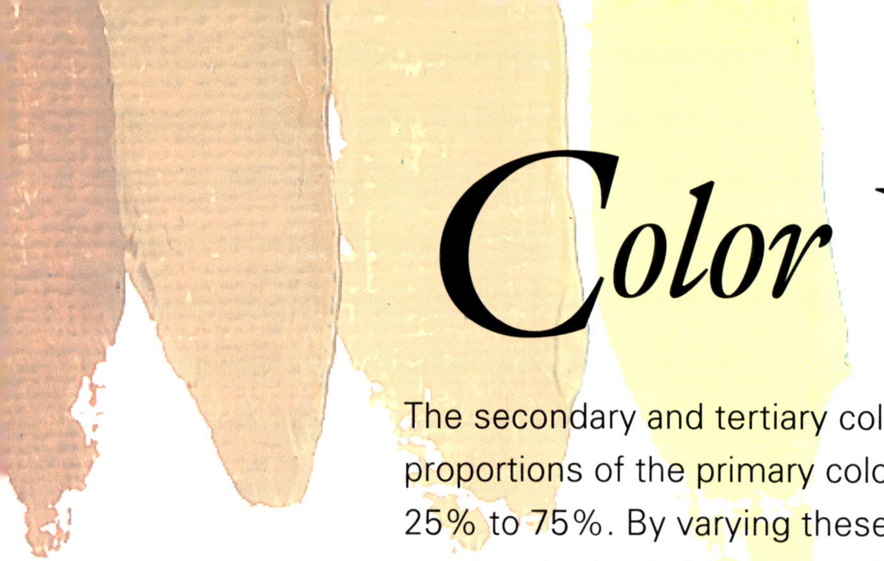

Color Variety I

The secondary and tertiary colors were obtained from definite proportions of the primary colors: in equal parts, or in a ratio of 25% to 75%. By varying these proportions, many more colors can be obtained. Moreover, if all the colors on the suggested palette are used for mixing, the possibilities are greatly multiplied.

Ranges from the Three Primary Colors

Producing ranges from two colors is an excellent practical exercise. It is even easier to carry out than to explain. In painting, a range is any ordered series of colors.

Start with two colors and deposit them on a clean part of your palette. The first mixture is made with a great amount of paint of the first color and very little of the second. Using this mixture, paint a first patch. For the second mix, add a little more of the second color and adjust. Paint a second patch with this mixture next to the first patch. This procedure is repeated until the last patch has much more of the second color than of the first.

1. A range mixed from yellow and crimson in varied proportions. The yellow and the crimson are at the two ends of the range.

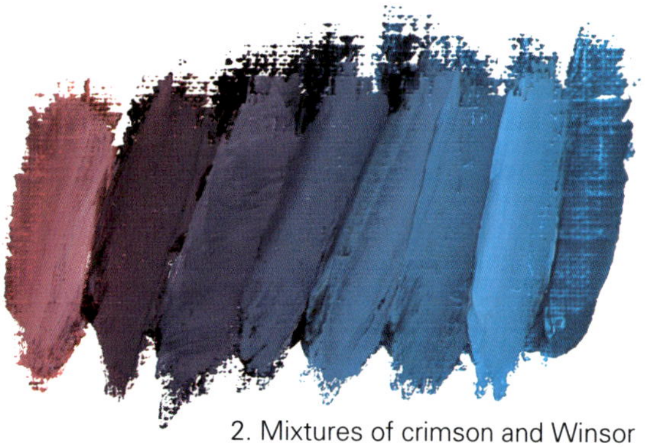

2. Mixtures of crimson and Winsor Blue in varied proportions. The mixture of crimson and blue gives a very dark range that can be lightened by adding a little white.

3. Mixing yellow and blue and varying the proportions. From basic yellow and blue, this attractive range of greens has been created.

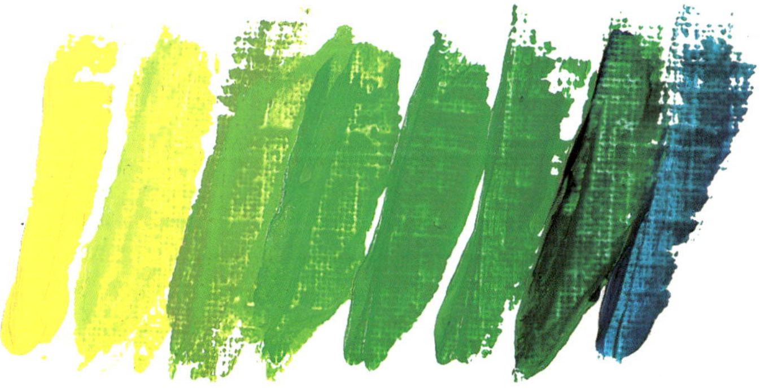

Ranges Using Other Colors on the Palette

Besides the three primary colors: yellow, crimson, and blue, in the suggested palette on pages 6 and 7, vermilion, Permanent Green Light, Chromium Oxide Green, and ultramarine also appear. With these colors, several different ranges can also be produced. While 90% of all colors can be mixed using the three primary colors, it is evident that, in practice, the use of all the colors on the suggested palette substantially enriches the mixtures, achieving a wide and rich range of color possibilities.

4. Yellow and the red from the palette. With yellow and vermilion a beautiful range of orange is achieved.

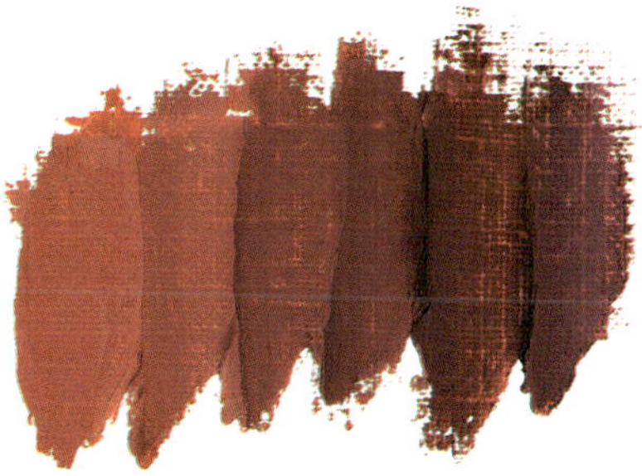

5. Intense reds are obtained by mixing crimson and vermilion.

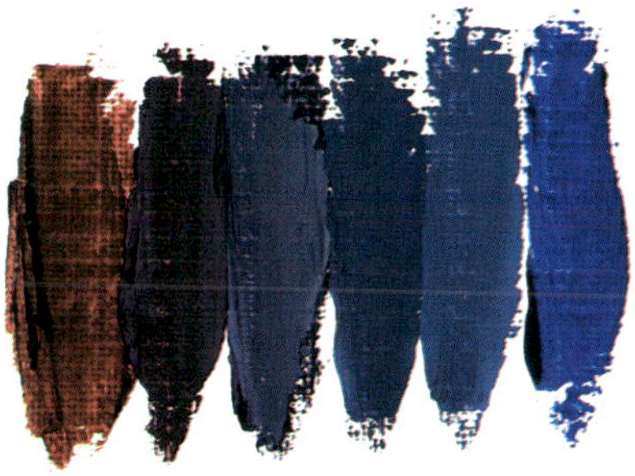

6. A dark violet range results from crimson and ultramarine.

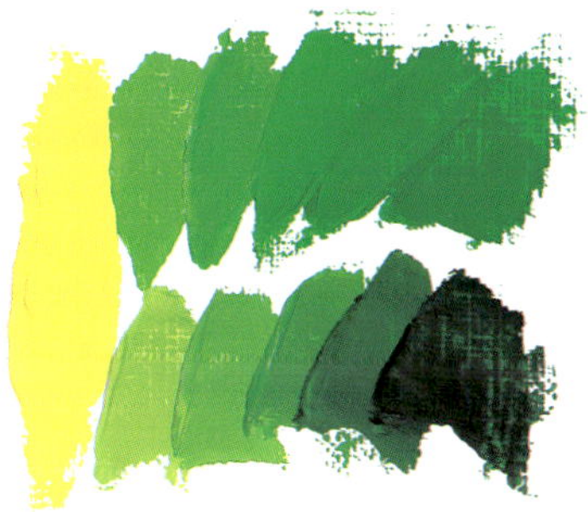

7. These lovely yellows are made up from yellow and Permanent Green Light.

8. With yellow and Chromium Oxide Green, the greens are intense and darker.

9. Starting with Permanent Green Light and Winsor Blue we obtain blue-greens.

10. With Permanent Green Light and ultramarine the blue-greens are darker.

11. This time by mixing yellow and ultramarine, more greens are obtained.

12. We get another range of blue-greens by mixing Chromium Oxide Green and Winsor Blue.

13. When Chromium Oxide Green and ultramarine are mixed, the blue-greens are darker and more intense.

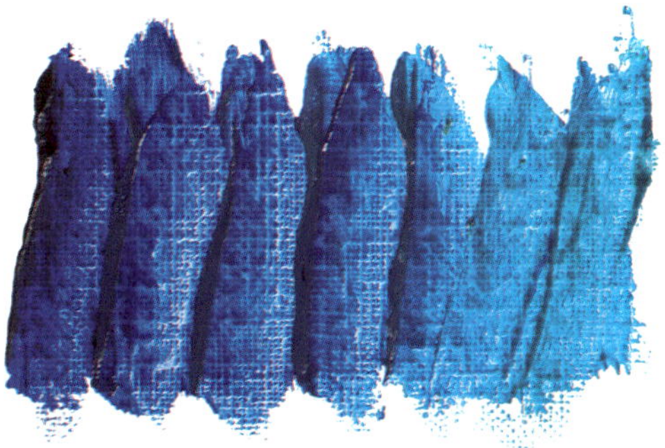

14. Lastly, by mixing the two blues on the palette the range of blues is extended.

REMEMBER...

- Ranges 4 and 5 extend range 1.
- Ranges 6 and 14 extend range 2.
- Ranges 7, 8, 9, 10, 11, 12, and 13 extend range 3.
- The earth colors, ochre, sienna, and umber are dealt with on pages 26 and 27.
- The ranges obtained using white appear on pages 28 and 29.
- The mixtures using black are on pages 30 and 31.

Color Variety 2

The earth colors, ochre, sienna, and umber, are colors that need special attention. Remember that they are broken colors. As such, their appearance is grayish and colors mixed with them will have that same aspect.

Neutral Colors Using Primary Colors

Neutral colors can be obtained by mixing the three primary colors, crimson, blue, and yellow. It is best to get used to taking up different amounts of paint by guesswork and work with the mixture until you get the color you are looking for. Let's start by creating ochre, sienna, and umber by mixing primary colors.

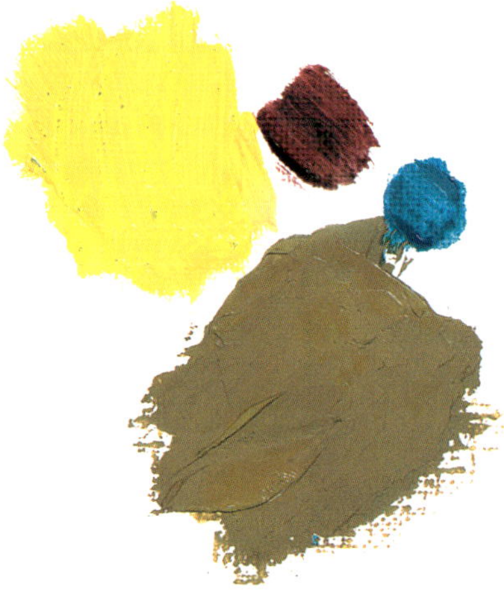

The Mix for Ochre

To obtain ochre from three primary colors, a lot of yellow is mixed with a little crimson and very little Winsor Blue.

To Obtain Sienna

An earth color similar to burnt sienna can be created by blending yellow and crimson in equal parts and adding a tiny amount of Winsor Blue as well.

To Make Umber

The earth color achieved by mixing crimson and Winsor Blue in equal quantities, and toning it with a little yellow, is very dark. This mixture is very like the umber on the suggested palette.

REMEMBER...

- All the earth colors are neutral or broken colors.
- If you mix any of the colors on the palette with an earth color, you will obtain another neutral color.
- The earth color called umber is very dark, almost black. It can successfully be used to tone down color. Use in very small amounts to neutralize color while not completely negating it.

Neutral Colors

When mixing an earth color (whether it be yellow ochre, sienna, or umber) with any other of the colors on your palette, bear in mind that it provides its share of yellow, crimson, and blue to the mixture.

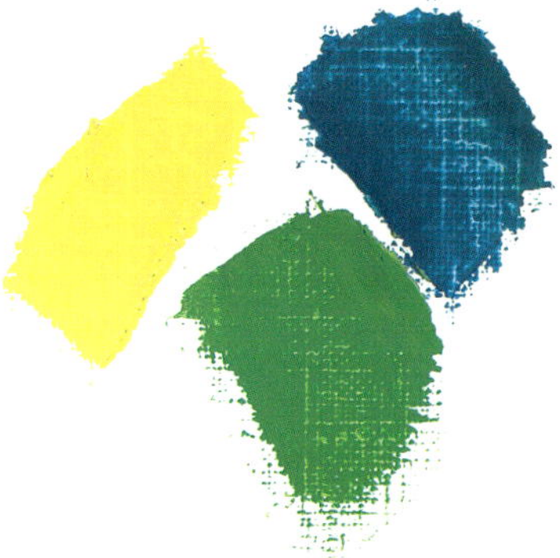

By mixing yellow and Winsor Blue in equal parts, we obtain green.

If we mix ochre and Winsor Blue, the green we get is darker and grayer. This is another neutral color, after all, because the mixture is made up of the three primary colors in unequal amounts.

Using Ochre as a Yellow

Ochre contains a lot of yellow; when it is mixed with another color you must remember that, besides yellow, it also contains a slight amount of blue and some crimson.

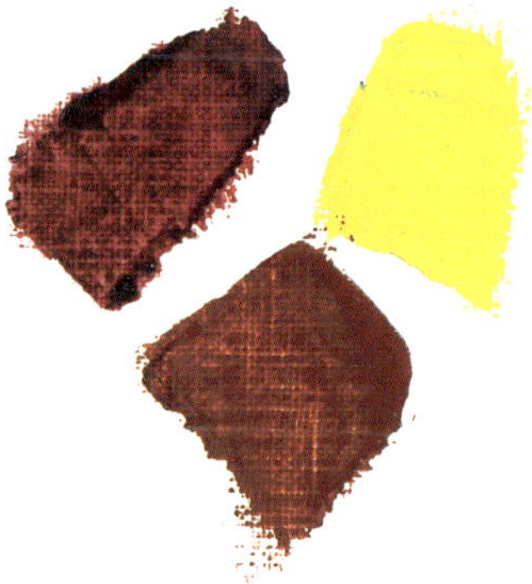

Yellow and crimson in equal parts form a secondary red.

Using Sienna as a Red

When you mix yellow and crimson in equal parts you obtain a secondary red. If you then add a little Winsor Blue you get an earth color similar to sienna. When you mix sienna with other colors, you are adding its red, its yellow, and its little bit of blue. Vermilion, crimson, and sienna are the three red colors on your palette. See what happens when you mix them with yellow.

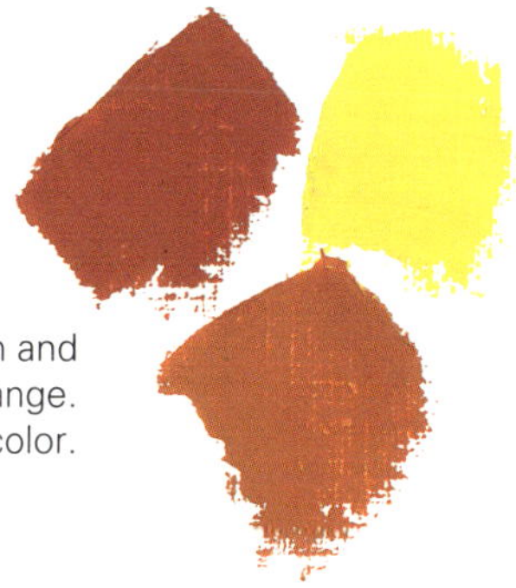

Equal parts of vermilion and yellow make an orange. A lovely tertiary color.

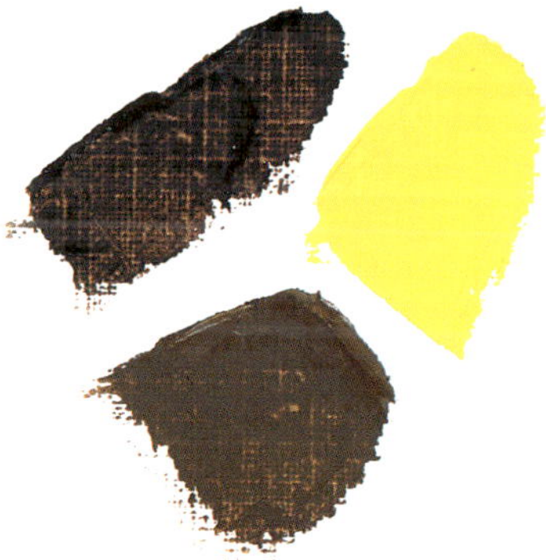

Mixing sienna and yellow in equal parts gives us a lighter, more golden color than the sienna. If the sienna carries as much yellow as the crimson, on mixing with yellow, the total amount of yellow is increased. The neutral color obtained from the mixture looks necessarily more golden.

Careful with Umber

Umber is a very strong, dark color and should be used in small amounts. Look at a few examples.

A lot of red and a little umber gives us a beautiful baked clay color.

Red and umber together make a very dark, undefinable color. Again, it is important to take care with the darkening effect of umber, using it in small quantities.

Grading with White

A range of grades or tones can be obtained with any color. The word "tone" means the degree of intensity of light. White will create gradations or ranges of light tones or tints of colors. A complete range of tones runs from the lightest, and least intense, to the darkest, and most intense. By mixing a color with white, and varying the proportions, light tones or tints are achieved.

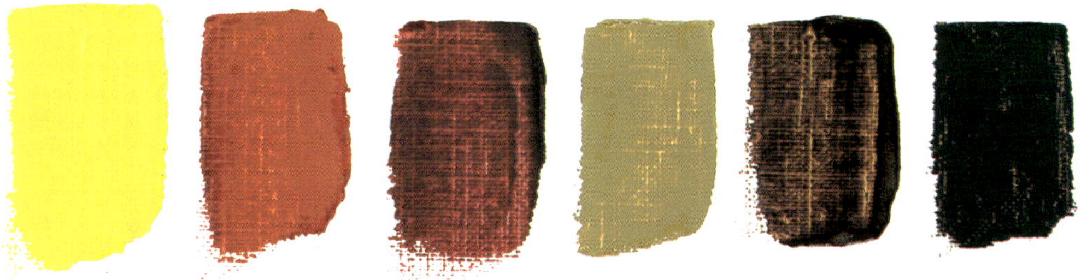

In order to produce the ranges of tone for the light colors that appear on these pages, all the colors on the palette have been used.

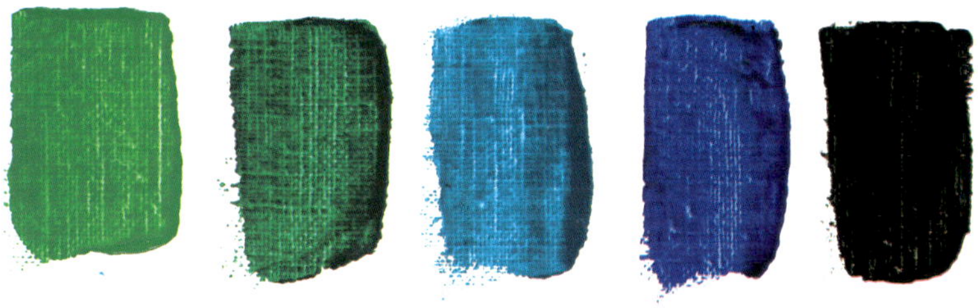

White-Producing Tones

By adding white, a color's intensity is reduced and it becomes opaque. The gradations that can be achieved using this method are extensive, with the exception of yellow, which fades out to white very quickly.

Note the following examples of short ranges. In each group of patches, the top represents the unmixed color. In the middle the color appears mixed with 50% white. And below, in the lightest tone, the quantity of white has been increased to 90%.

Two points should be remembered: first that wider ranges of colors can be obtained by varying the proportions of white, and second, a tonal gradation with white can be produced for any of the colors on the palette.

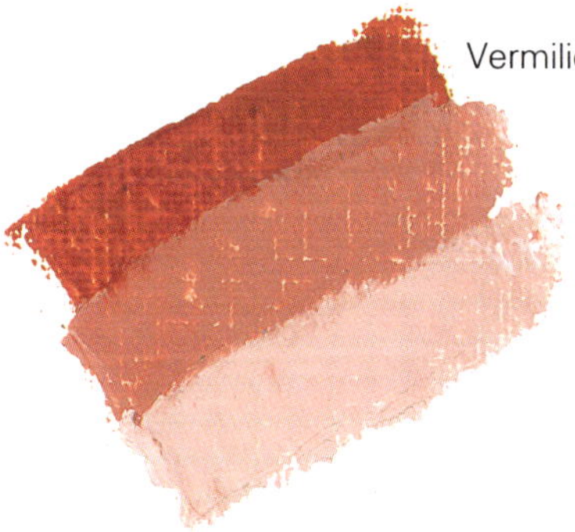

Vermilion and white

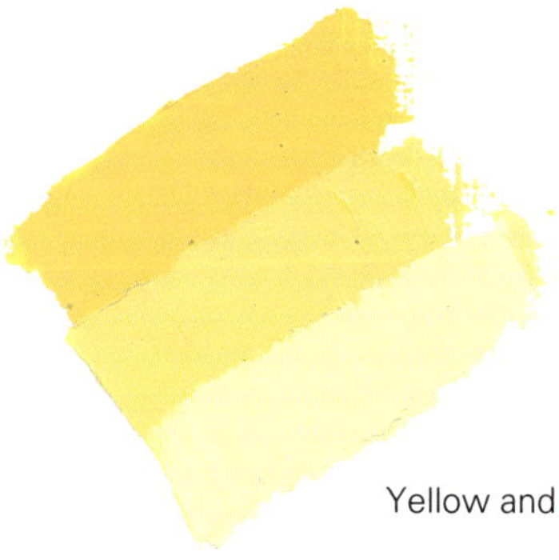

Yellow and white

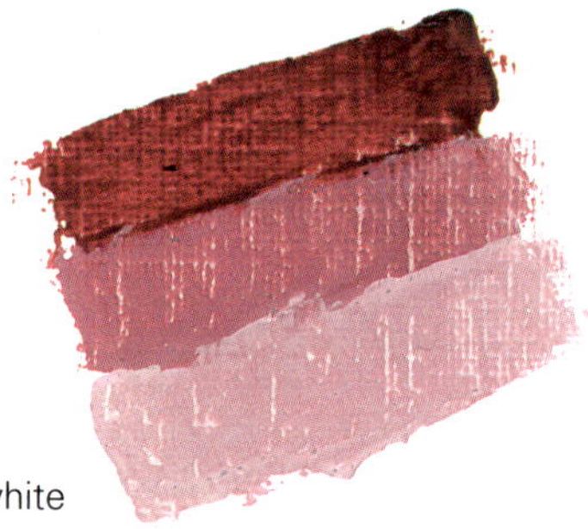

Crimson and white

Ochre and white.

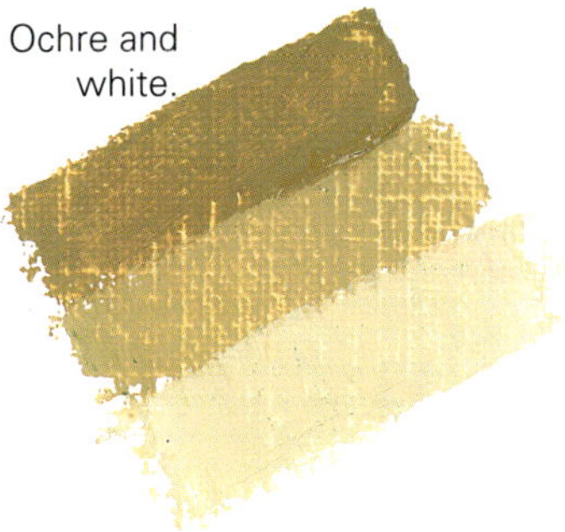

Burnt Sienna and white.

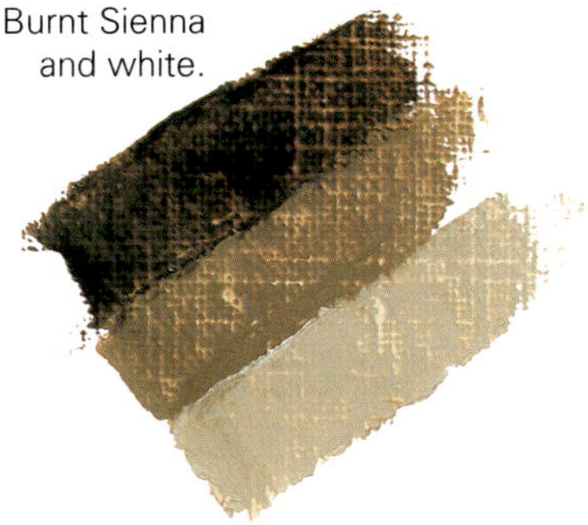

Burnt Umber and white.

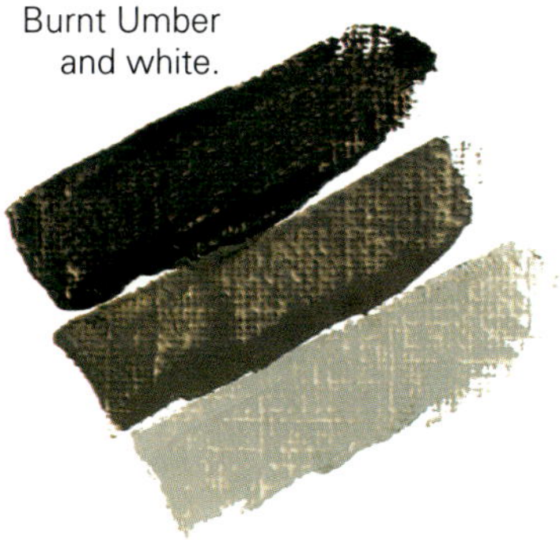

Permanent Green Light and white.

Chromium Oxide Green and white.

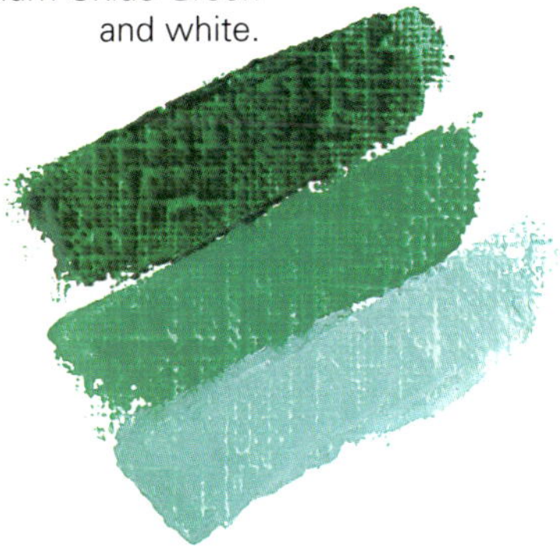

Winsor Blue and white.

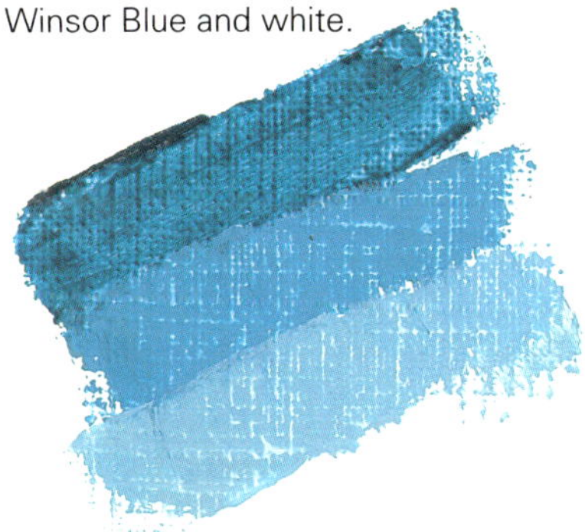

Ultramarine and white.

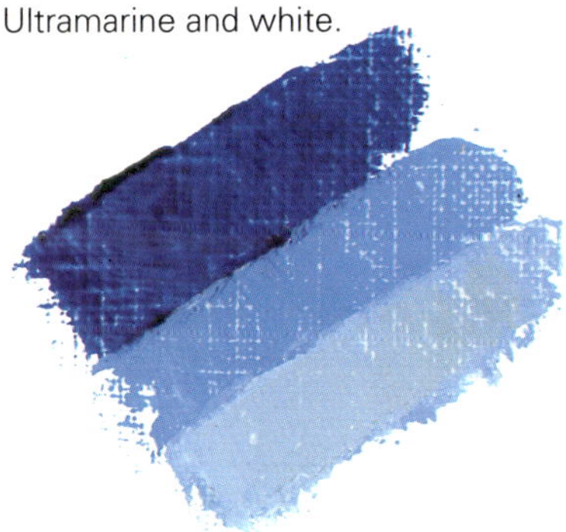

REMEMBER...

- White needs to be used with other colors in order to create light opaque tones.
- In good color grading there are no jumps from one tone to another, however big the surface may be.
- Colors change when white is added. For this reason, one of oil painting's secrets is to use as little white as possible when mixing. Consult pages 34 and 35 about related colors for more information on this.
- White, apart from lightening colors, also gives them a grayish tinge.

Graded Color: An Example

It is important to learn how to use grays for creating tones of color. By mixing black with white and varying the proportions, we can create a range of grays. In Figure 1, brushstrokes have been painted side by side of different shades of diminishing intensities of grays moving from left to right. In Figure 2, the grading has been carried out without jumping from one shade to the next by blending the consecutive tones with a paintbrush and/or the finger.

In order to get a good gradation, every time you move on from one tone to the next you should use a clean paintbrush or finger to keep the tones clean.

1. Range of tones of gray using black and white.

2. Grading down from black.

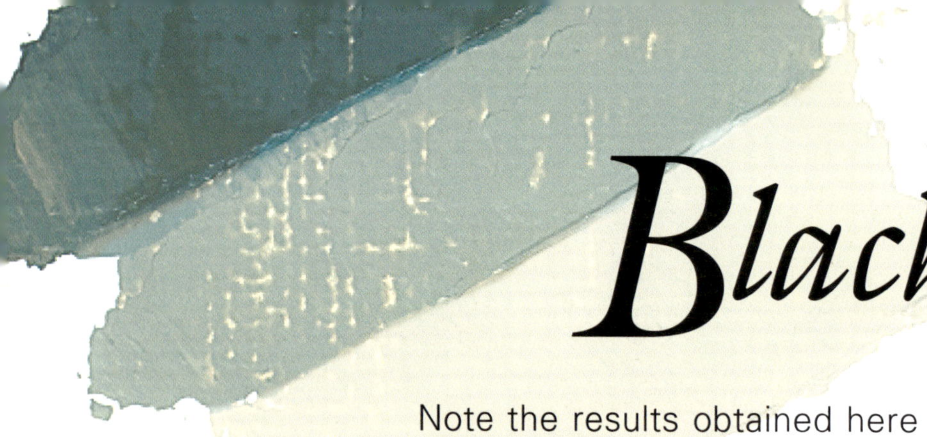

Black

Note the results obtained here when colors are darkened by mixing them with black. It can be seen, for example, that yellow tends toward green, and red tends toward brown. In general, all the dark colors appear muddy. In fact, the most effective way of darkening a color is by adding these mixed "blacks."

In order to create the examples of darkening colors by adding black that appear on this page, the following palette has been used as a starting point (from left to right): yellow, vermilion, crimson, ochre, and sienna.

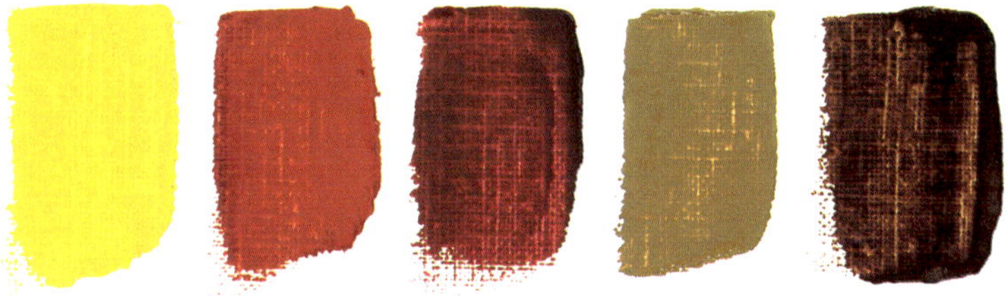

Black and Mixtures

When black is used to darken colors, the result is a change in the color, mixtures that appear muddy.

In each example shown, the first color to appear is the unmixed original color. Below, the next patch of color, of a darker shade, is obtained by mixing the color with a little black, 20% or so. The darkest patch corresponds to the greatest proportion of black, about 50%.

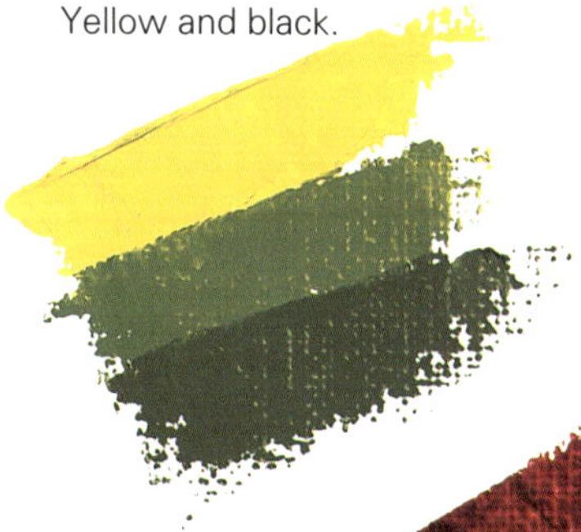

Yellow and black.

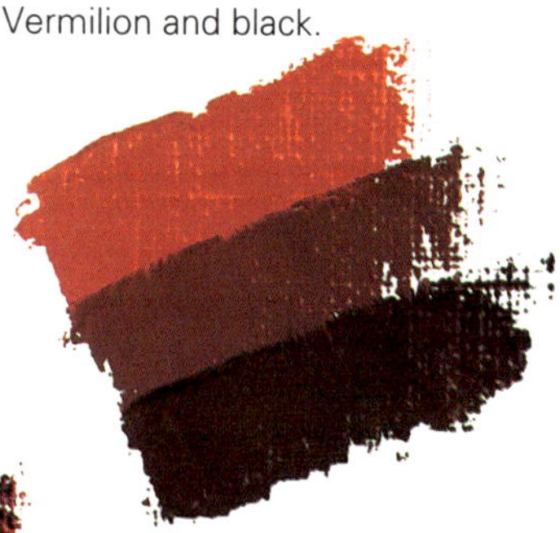

Vermilion and black.

Crimson and black.

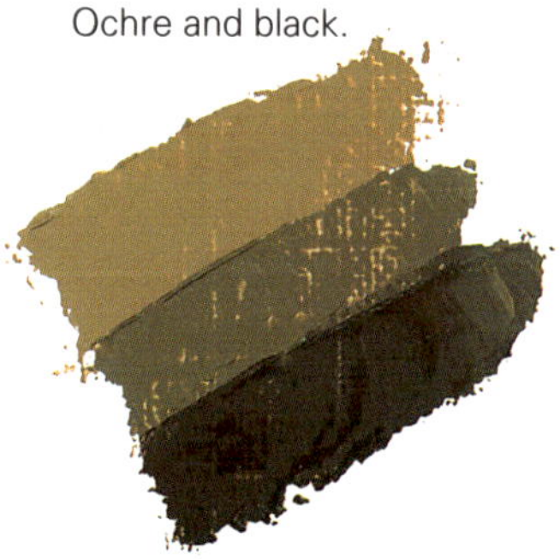

Ochre and black.

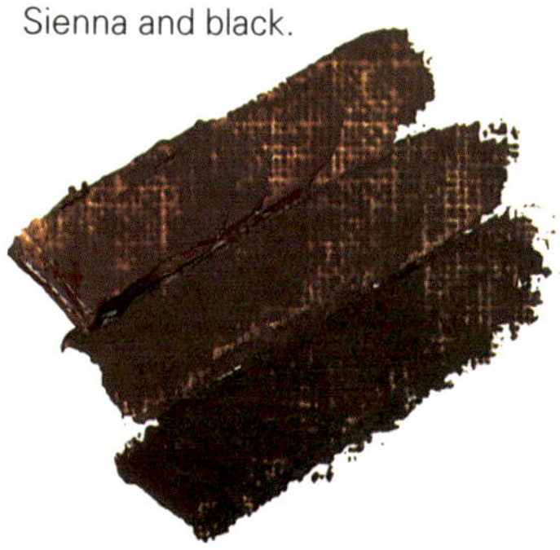

Sienna and black.

REMEMBER...

- Black used in mixtures will tend to greatly negate color.
- A color can be darkened with darker tones of similar colors or by means of variable "blacks" with less negation of hue. This point will be discussed thoroughly on pages 34 and 35.

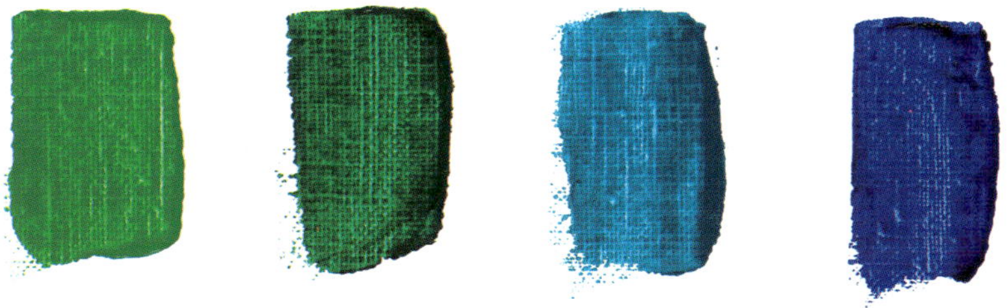

Here black is added to the cool colors on the palette (from left to right): Permanent Green Light, Chromium Oxide Green, Winsor Blue, and ultramarine.

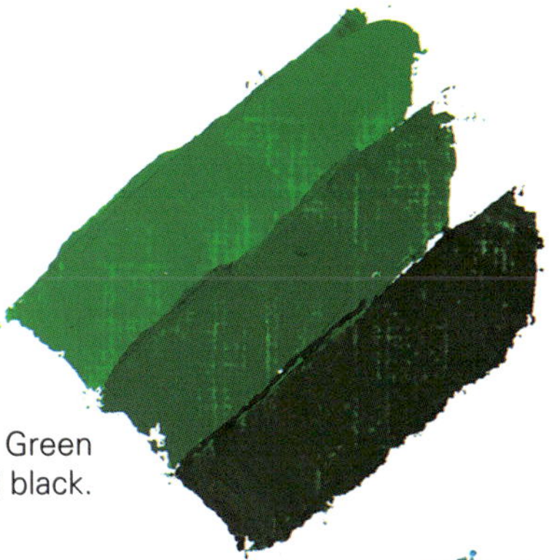

Permanent Green Light and black.

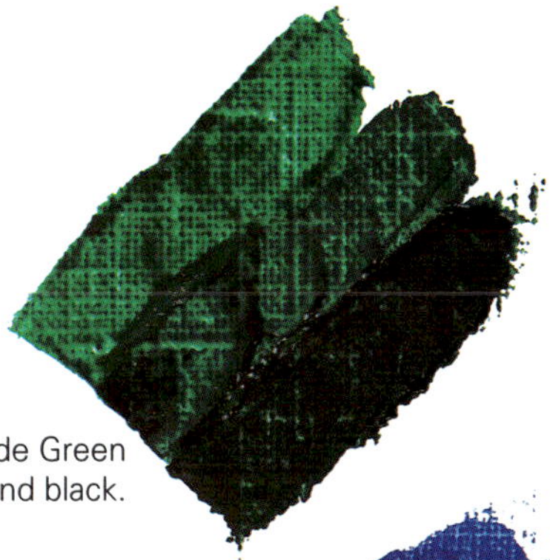

Chromium Oxide Green and black.

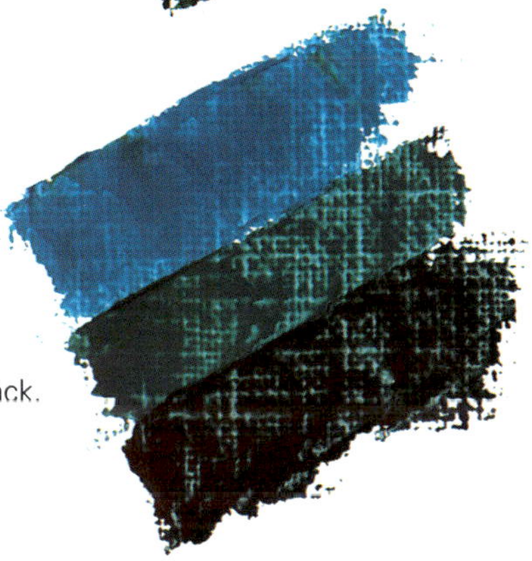

Winsor Blue and black.

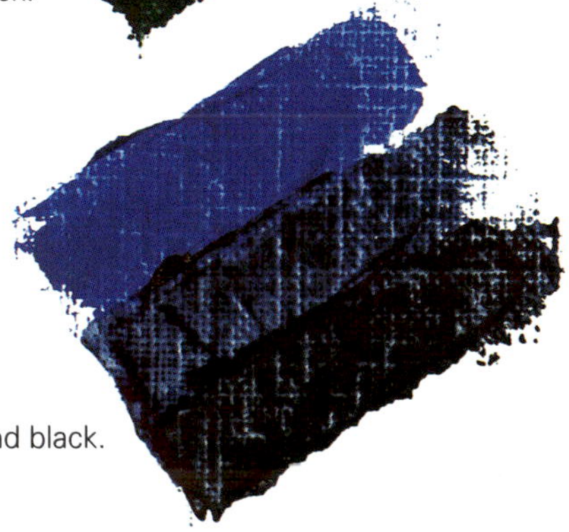

Ultramarine and black.

Variable "Blacks"

Among the possibilities of our suggested palette, very dark colors can be obtained by means of mixtures. If you mix crimson, Chromium Oxide Green, and umber in equal parts, a very dark color results. Similarly, when you mix crimson, Chromium Oxide Green, and ultramarine in equal parts, the color you get is also very dark.

If, instead of mixing in equal parts, you allow one color to predominate over the other two, then the dark color has a hue, that of the predominant color. For instance, if you use more ultramarine your "black" will have a blue cast to it. These "blacks" can be varied and will enrich any piece of work with more tones.

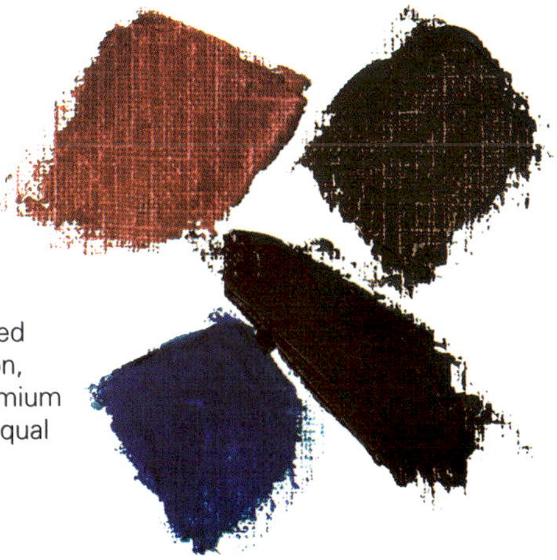

A "black" obtained by mixing crimson, umber, and Chromium Oxide Green in equal parts.

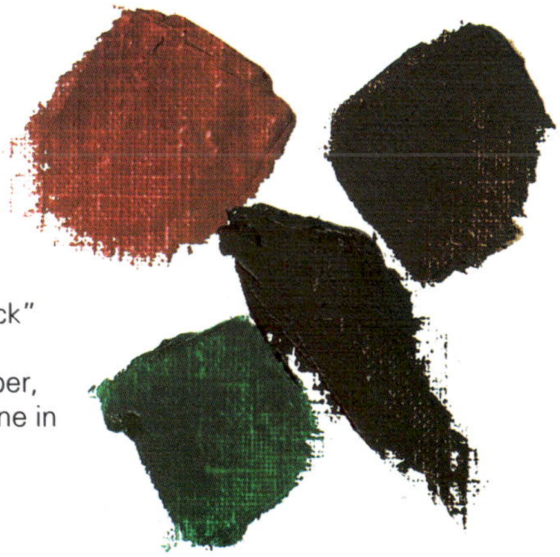

Another "black" created from crimson, umber, and ultramarine in equal parts.

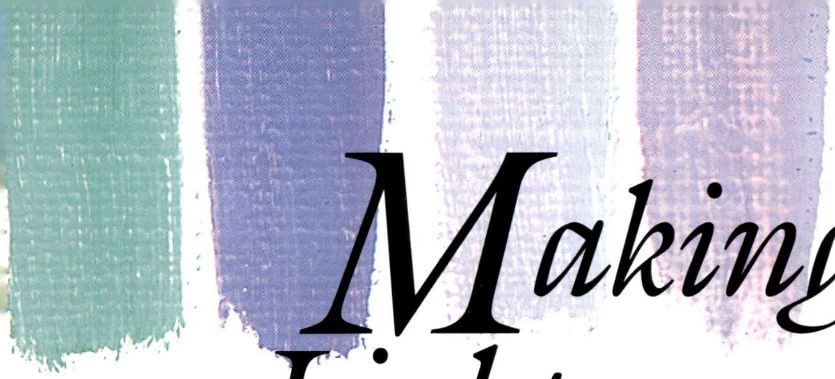

Making Colors Lighter or Darker

In practice, when painting from reality, mixing tones, tints, and shades is required in order to model the illusion of volume. Look at some examples and see the limitations of lightening colors with white and darkening them using black. Here are some first exercises in representing everyday objects in oils. In each case a range of tones of one color is created.

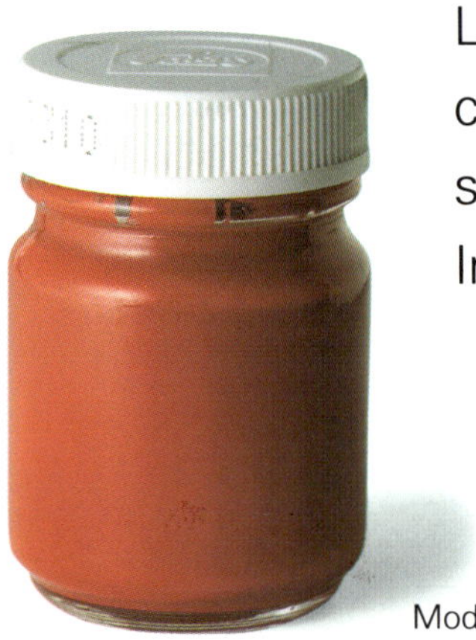

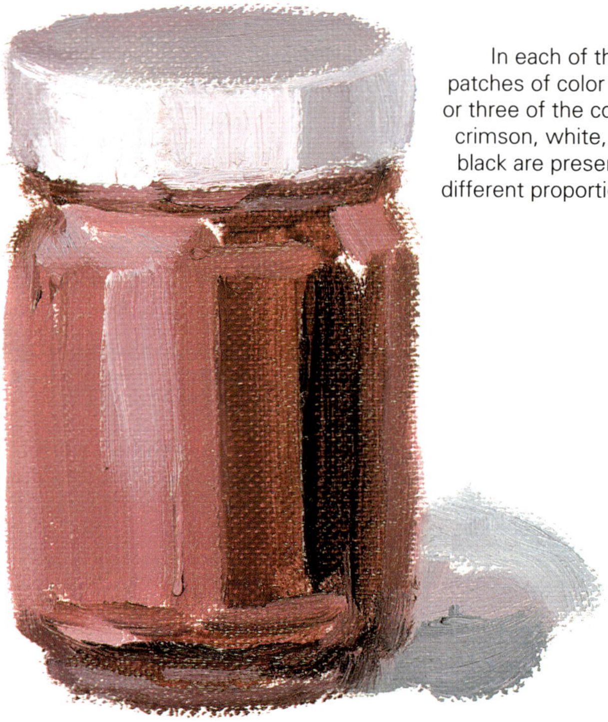

A jar.
Model and painting.

In each of these patches of color two or three of the colors crimson, white, and black are present in different proportions.

Crimson

If crimson is lightened with white and darkened with black, the color is monochromatic and gray.

In the photograph, the jar shows a clear vertical band of crimson on the right. Lightening the crimson with white only produces pink and not the red we need. On darkening the crimson with a little black, a dull undefined mixture is obtained. The resulting painting has nothing of the original's color richness.

REMEMBER...

- Lightening and darkening a color with white and black tends to dull color.
- Crimson tends toward pink when white is added, and toward muddy brown on adding black.

Range for the lid. All three colors, crimson, white, and black, are present.

Range of crimson lightened with white and darkened with black.

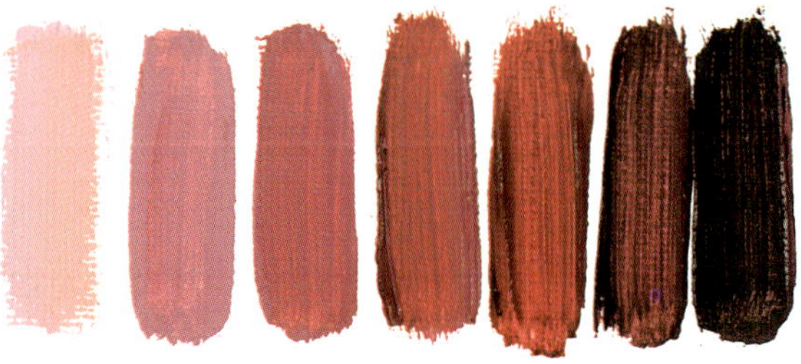

Blue

To paint this cigarette lighter, we have used unmixed Winsor Blue for the side surface. The two lighter shades of blue are obtained by adding white in two different proportions, while the darker blue is the result of adding a touch of black. This dark blue appears dull and gray. Also, the reflections on the metal are represented by mixtures of all three colors: a lot of white, a little blue, and very little black. Despite trying to obtain tones, the aspect is dull and gray.

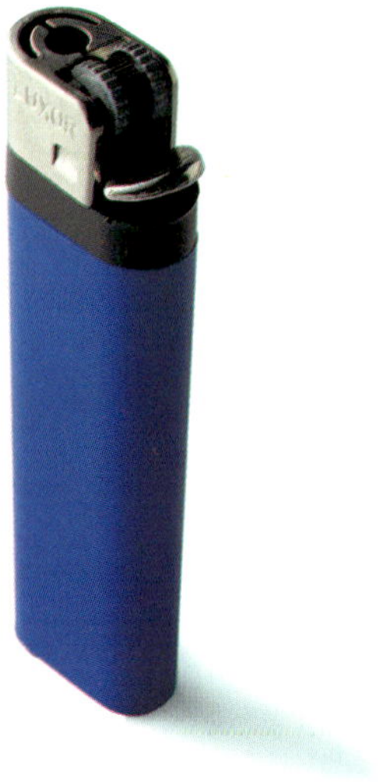

Model and painting.

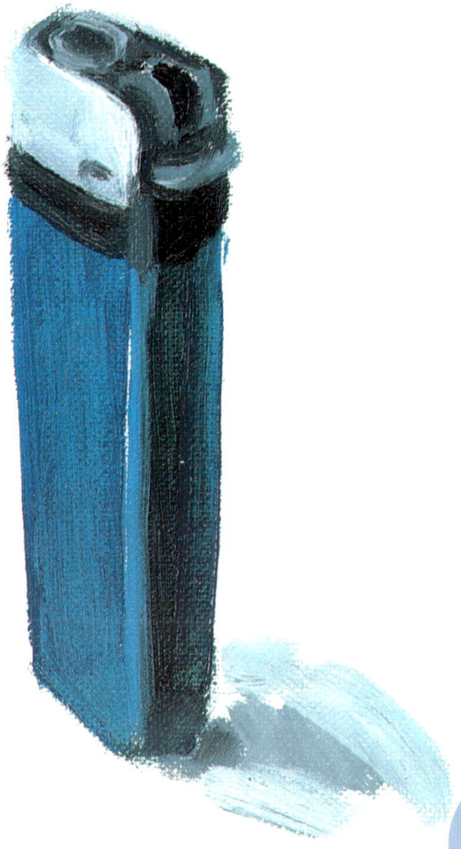

Range for the blue parts of the model.

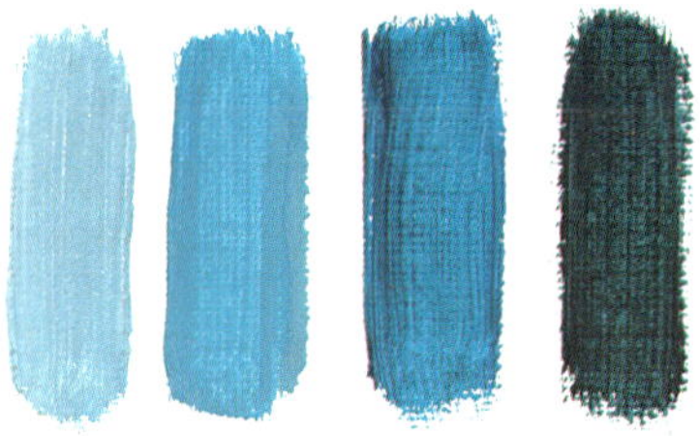

Range for the grays on the top part of the lighter.

Yellow

The lightest shades of yellow are obtained by mixing with white in different proportions. To darken the yellow, we will use black. The more black we add to the yellow, the greener and muddier the resulting mixture is.

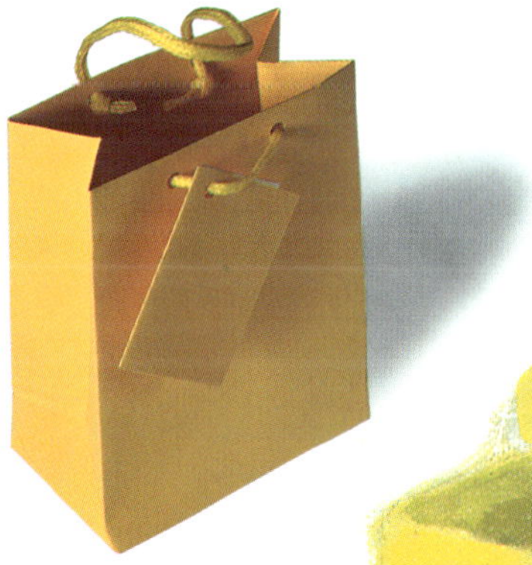

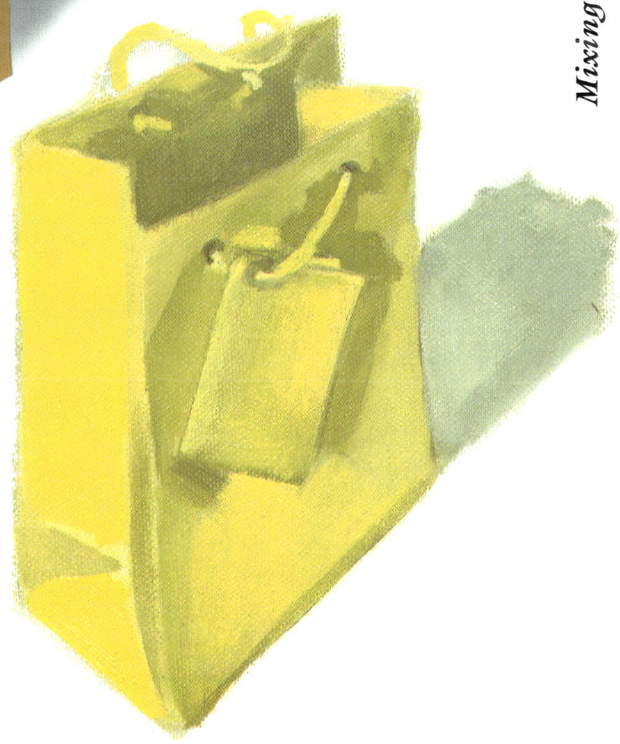

Range using yellow, white, and black used to paint the paper bag.

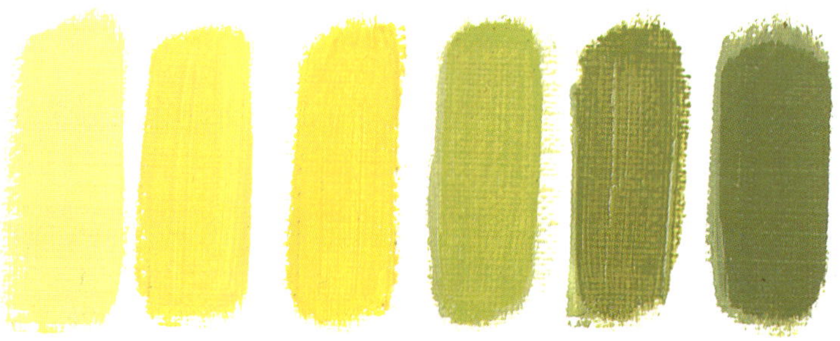

Grading with Related Colors

The way to avoid color changes when creating different tones is to use related colors.

The color **Light Cadmium Yellow** can be lightened with other, lighter, yellows, white, or with a mixture of these. In turn, it can be darkened with darker yellows and even with a touch of red, ochre, or mixtures of these.

Vermilion can be lightened with white, yellows, all the lighter reds, or their mixtures. It can be darkened with darker reds or their mixtures. On our suggested palette crimson darkens vermilion.

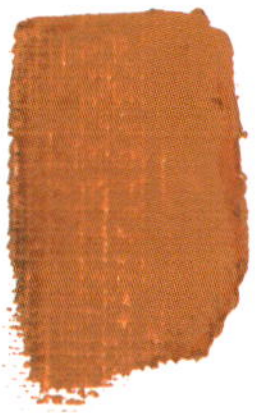

Crimson can be lightened with white, yellows, all the lighter reds, or their mixtures. Crimson is the darkest in the group of reds, but it can be darkened with ultramarine, umber or Chromium Oxide Green.

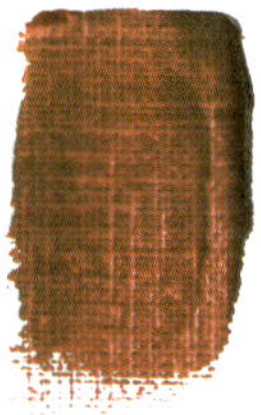

Ochre can be lightened with white, yellows, or their mixtures. It can be progressively darkened with burnt sienna and then with burnt umber.

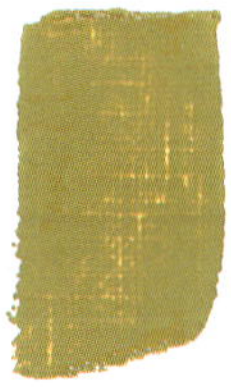

Sienna can be lightened with mixtures of white, yellows, and reds. It is usually darkened with burnt umber. Redder shades can be obtained by increasing its red content, or darker shades by adding blues.

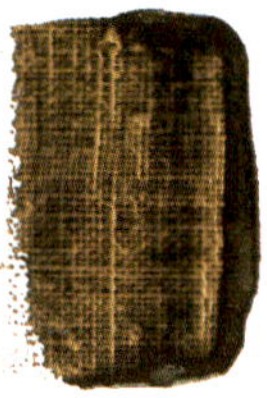

In the case of **burnt umber**, this is lightened with white, yellows, reds and lighter neutrals, or their mixtures. While being one of the brown colors, it is the darkest of all and the color used to darken other browns.

Permanent Green Light can be lightened with white and yellows and darkened with Chromium Oxide Green and the blues.

Chromium Oxide Green can be lightened with white, yellows, and medium green.

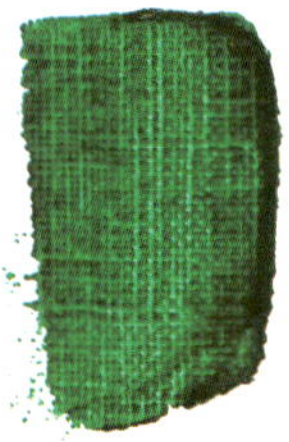

Winsor Blue can be lightened with white and darkened with ultramarine. A little crimson can also be added (remember how secondary deep blue is formed).

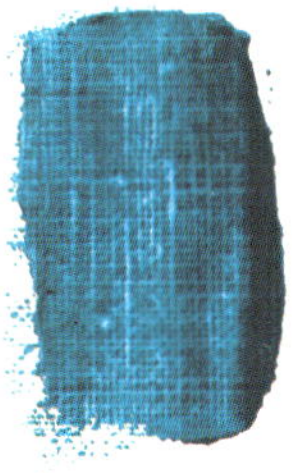

Ultramarine can be lightened with white and Winsor Blue.

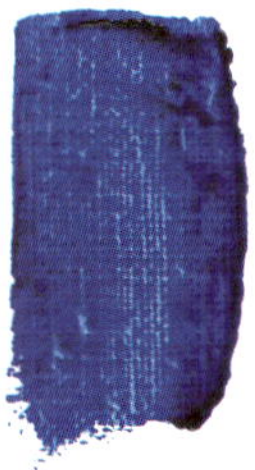

Related Colors

The colors related to one specific color are found among the colors included in its group. The groups, again, are the yellows, the reds, the neutrals, the greens, the blues, and the browns. Within each group the lighter colors (or their mixtures) lighten the darker ones while the darker colors (or their mixtures) darken the lighter ones.

On a palette with the colors arranged in the order we've pictured on pages 10 and 11, from cool to warm, the colors (or their mixture) that lighten are warmer while those that darken are cooler.

Variable "Blacks" for Darkening

Variable "blacks" can effectively be used for mixing a color's darkest shade. A greater amount of one of three colors, the one nearest to the color we wish to darken, must be used. For example, if we are darkening a red with a variable "black" we would use one mixed of crimson, umber, and blue and use a greater amount of crimson.

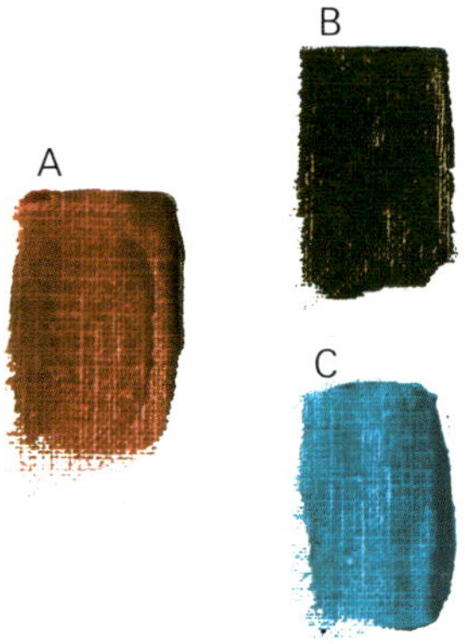

A. If crimson dominates, the black will have a crimson hue.

B. A "black" mixed from crimson, umber, and blue

C. If blue predominates, the black will have a bluish hue.

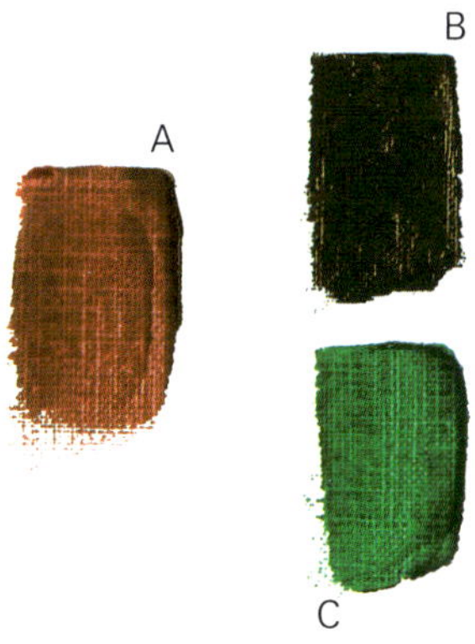

A. If crimson predominates, the black will have a crimson hue.

B. A "black" mixed from crimson, umber, and Chromium Oxide Green.

C. If Chromium Oxide Green predominates, the "black" will be a greenish brown.

Color Has to Be Created

In any illuminated object, we observe its color in several tones. Each of these is a mixture that we have to create. Going back to the example of the jar of red on page 32: now the vermilion can be lightened with yellow and a little white. It can be progressively darkened by adding crimson (up to 50%), and by adding 20% of Winsor Blue to the crimson in order to obtain the darkest red.

What's the Color Like?

This is the fundamental question and the answer has to be found each time we want to mix a new color. It is always a question of comparing tonal relationships. To put it simply, one color is lighter or darker than another. The hue, or color, is also very important. Here the painter's ability to observe comes into play. There are yellowish, orange, pinkish, golden, reddish, crimson, violet, bluish, greenish, grayish hues...as well as a great number of others. For each shade, the mixture has to be made up of correspondingly related colors.

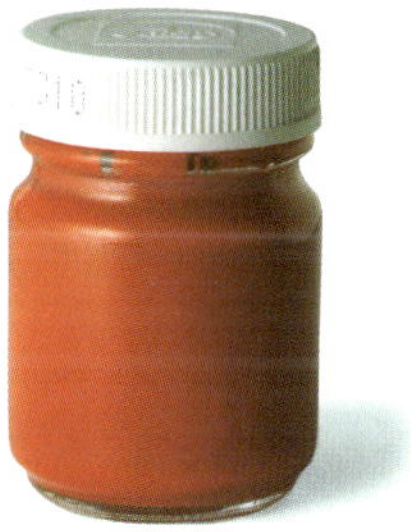

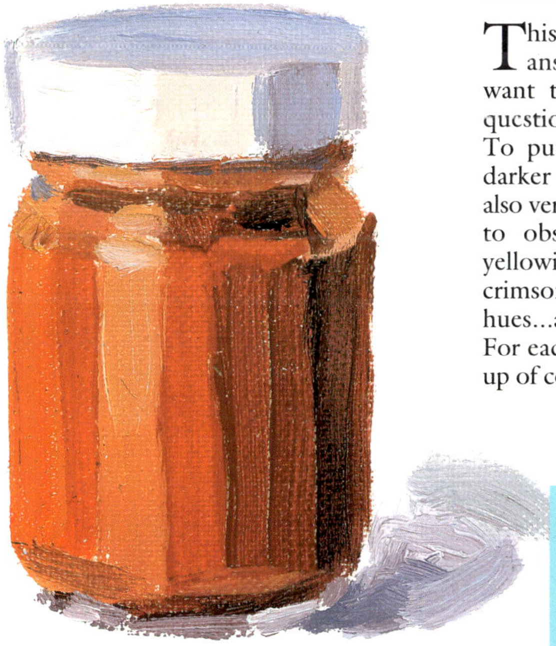

Model and painting.

Mixtures used to paint the jar of red paint.

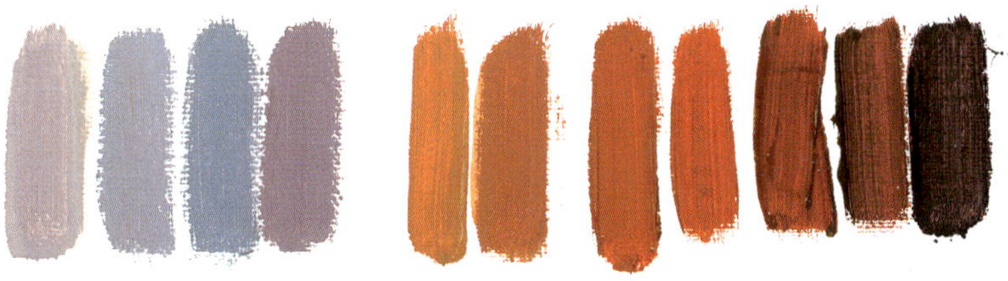

REMEMBER...

- We recommend lightening and darkening colors and mixtures of color using related colors or mixtures rather than using black.
- A painting in which the mixtures have been lightened or darkened using related colors or mixtures is rich in tones.
- With the ability to observe, and applying the theory of color and some common sense, mixing colors only requires practice.

Crimson Mixed with Other Colors

Keep experimenting with the palette of colors. To discover all its possibilities it is a good idea to mix a color with each of the others. The two examples chosen, crimson on these pages, and blue on the two following pages, will help to introduce the concept of harmony among colors.

We have chosen crimson to demonstrate mixing with each of the rest of the colors. Alizarin Crimson is a color that is used with great frequency as it is an effective color for mixing [for obtaining] oranges and reds (as well as a full range of violets). So, crimson is a good color to practice with.

Mixing Crimson with Other Colors

Whenever you mix crimson with other colors, you should remember the basic theoretical proportions of 50% and 50% to obtain a secondary color and 75% and 25% to obtain a tertiary color. You should also be especially careful with complementary colors, using unequal proportions in order to obtain strong neutral colors.

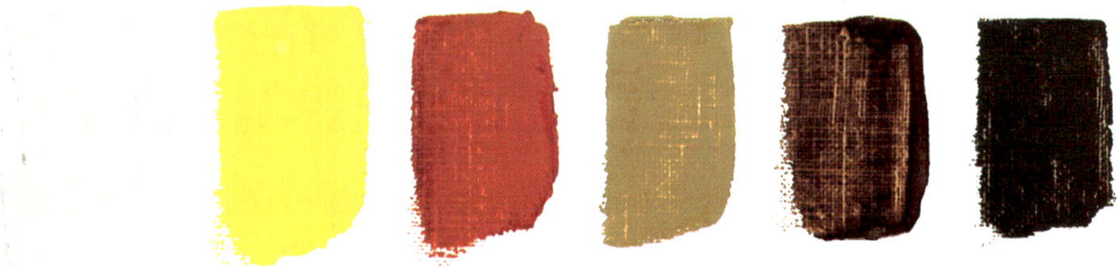

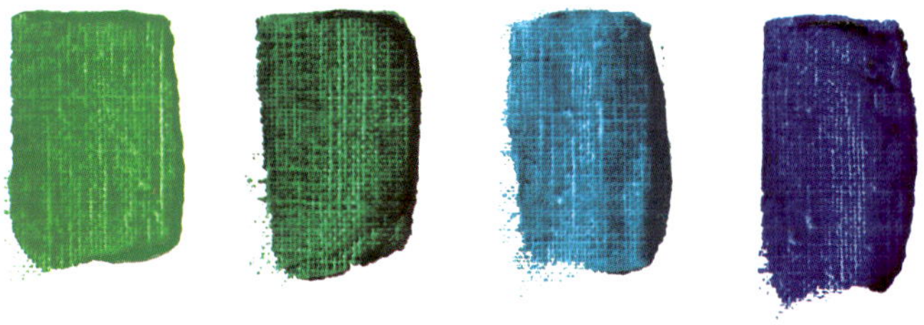

The following are the colors that are going to be mixed with crimson.

1. A mixture of crimson and white in equal parts. Note the bright pink with a crimson hue.

2. This mixture consists of 80% yellow and 20% crimson.

3. A deep red obtained from 40% vermilion and 60% crimson.

4. Ochre and crimson mixed in equal parts gives this lovely baked clay color.

5. If the same quantities of crimson and sienna are combined, a dark, crimson-hued earth color is obtained.

6. With umber (40%) and crimson (60%) a very dark color is obtained that still retains its crimson hue.

7. Here Permanent Green Light and crimson are blended in a ratio of 20% to 80%. A touch of white has been added to the mixture.

8. Chromium Oxide Green and crimson are complementary and will tend to negate each other, becoming gray. For this reason they should be mixed disproportionately, crimson dominating in quantity to which a tiny amount of green and a little white are added.

9. In this mixture there is 10% Winsor Blue and 90% crimson. A spot of white has been added afterwards.

10. A little ultramarine and a lot of crimson, together with a bit of white, gives another shade of cold crimson.

REMEMBER...

- Always ask yourself the question: How do I want the color to appear?
- Since all the color ingredients influence the final mixture, the composition and amounts of secondary and tertiary colors are important.
- Mixtures with complementary colors should be of very unequal amounts so that they do not negate their hues resulting in gray.

An Introduction to Harmony

The mixtures that appear on these two pages provide a pleasant or harmonious feeling. This is the basic principle of what is known as color harmony.

One method of creating color harmony in an oil painting consists of having a dominant color in all of the mixtures used in the painting (the dominant color here is Alizarin Crimson).

A warm hue, crimson, dominates these patches of color from 1 to 10. Though the contrast between the colors we started out mixing with is strong, within the set of the mixtures we created with them they have been toned down or harmonized.

Blue Mixed with Other Colors

The following is another practical exercise that consists of mixing a cool color, Winsor Blue, with the other colors on the suggested palette.

Here, Winsor Blue will be mixed with all the other colors. Just as crimson is a warm color, blue is a cool color. Note how this cool characteristic is manifest in each of the resulting mixtures.

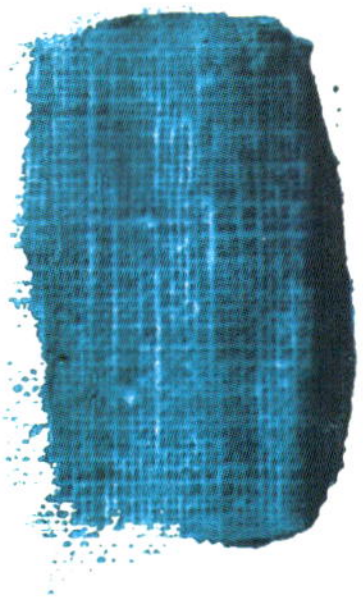

Mixing Blue with Other Colors

When mixing one color with any other, bear in mind that equal proportions give you a secondary color and using a 3 to 1 ratio gives you a tertiary color. Also remember that mixing complementary colors in unequal proportions results in strong neutral colors.

1. This beautiful light blue is obtained by mixing Winsor Blue with a small amount of white, about 20%.

REMEMBER...

- Blue is a cool color. Winsor Blue and ultramarine are the two coolest colors on the suggested palette.
- By mixing Winsor Blue with the yellows, greens, or blues on the palette, you get yellow-greens, greens, blue-greens, and blues.
- Blue with reds gives us purples, violets, and blue-violets.

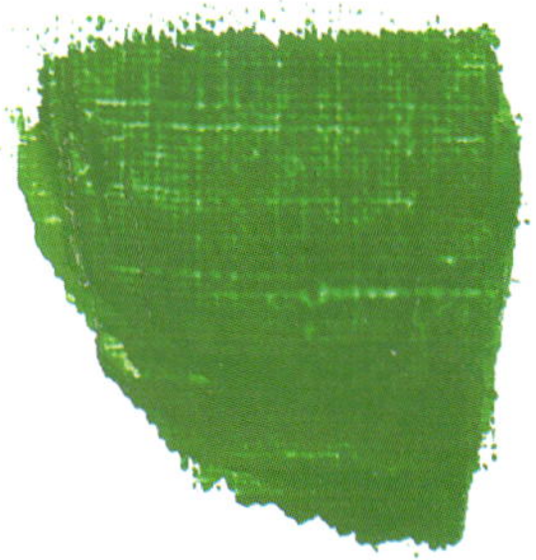

2. A bright green is obtained by mixing 40% yellow and 60% Winsor Blue.

3. A little red, just 10%, is added to the blue, as well as a touch of white. This is a very interesting, slightly neutral, blue color.

4. Here we have mixed 40% crimson and 60% Winsor Blue. This is a color halfway between secondary blue and tertiary blue.

5. Winsor Blue mixed with ochre, with a little more blue than ochre, gives us a beautiful neutral green.

6. With Winsor Blue, a little bit of sienna (approximately 10%), and a spot of white, we obtain a neutral blue-green.

7. Mixing Winsor Blue with a tiny amount of umber will tone it into a neutral, but magnificent, greenish blue.

8. By mixing Permanent Green Light and Winsor Blue in equal parts, you obtain a lovely cold green.

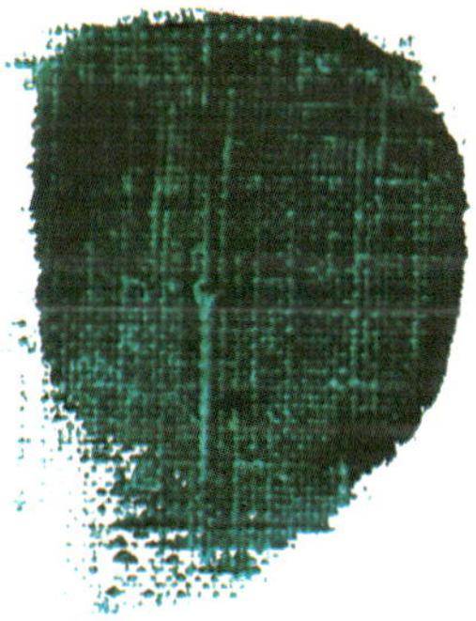

9. This intense blue-green is obtained by mixing Winsor Blue and Chromium Oxide Green in similar amounts.

10. Here is an intermediate shade of blue made by mixing equal parts of Winsor Blue and ultramarine.

Harmonizing

As you can see, all the mixtures that appear on these two pages make up a group of colors that appears pleasing to the eye. Each one is a cool hue. As a general rule, we have added smaller amounts of ochre colors to the blue in order to keep the mixtures weighted toward cool. The presence of blue in each of these mixtures tends to unify or harmonize them when seen together.

The Range of Warm Colors

The warm colors are the result of mixing reds and yellows. Painting in warm colors gives the illusion of warm, yellow light. The following is a palette suited to producing a subject with a profusion of yellows, reds, and earth colors bathed in warm midday light.

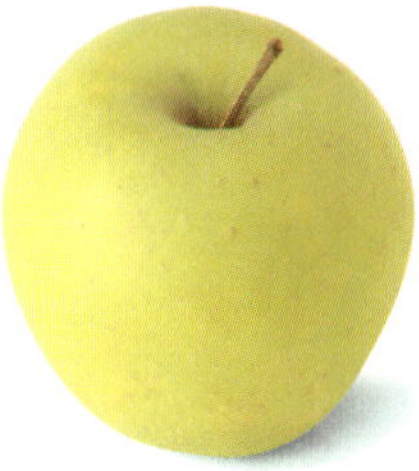

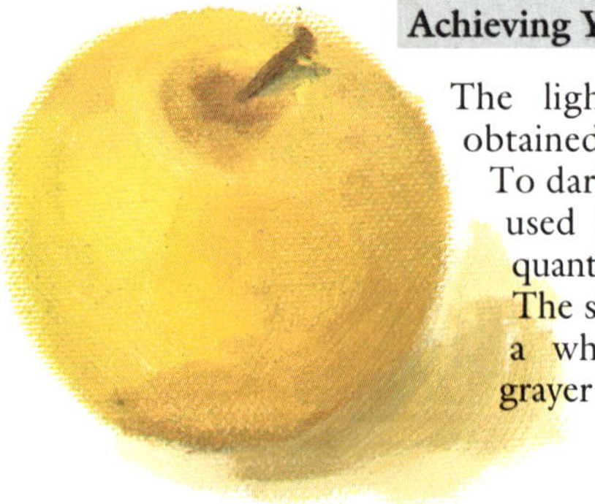

Achieving Yellow Tones

The lightest and brightest color is obtained by mixing white with yellow. To darken the yellow, ochre has been used followed by sienna in minute quantities in order to deepen the tone. The shadow of the apple, thrown on a white surface, presents slightly grayer shades of all the mixtures.

Achieving the Orange

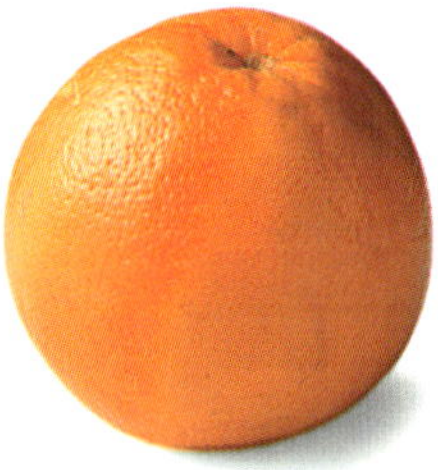

In order to paint the orange, we have used, basically, yellow, vermilion, and crimson. White is only used for the lightest brushstrokes. Winsor Blue is used, in very small amounts, only to deepen the tone of the shadows or the reflections. To create orange tones, remember the composition of the tertiary colors—yellow and vermilion are mixed in similar quantities. A touch more of yellow gives us an orange that approaches yellow, while using a bit more vermilion gives a reddish orange. Observe the shade, a broken orange tone, of the shadow that is cast.

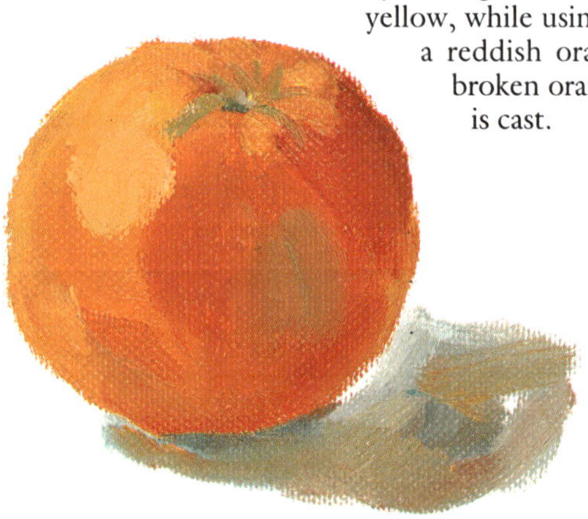

Creating Red

Starting with vermilion and crimson we can obtain these tomato reds. White and yellow are used in tiny amounts for the reflections and the lighter shades. Note the crimson tone of the shadow.

Create Ranges while Painting

Thanks to color, an object's volume can be represented on the flat surface of the canvas. The effect of volume is achieved by creating mixtures of differing shades.

The following exercises, all done in a range of warm colors, will help equip you to begin painting still life, using a full spectrum of color, cool to warm.

No object is ever painted in one color only. Its representation is composed of several brushstrokes of different tones and shades, and often of different hues and color groups.

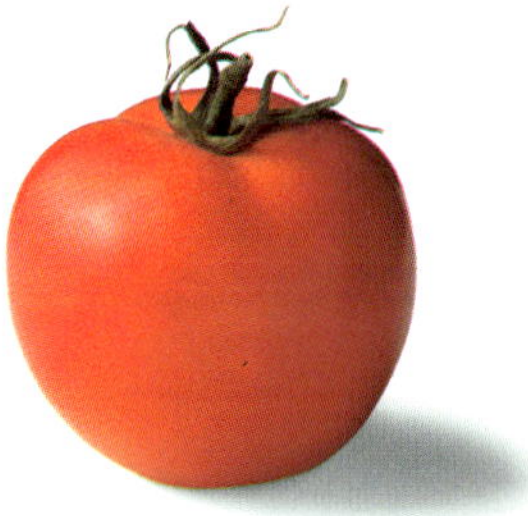

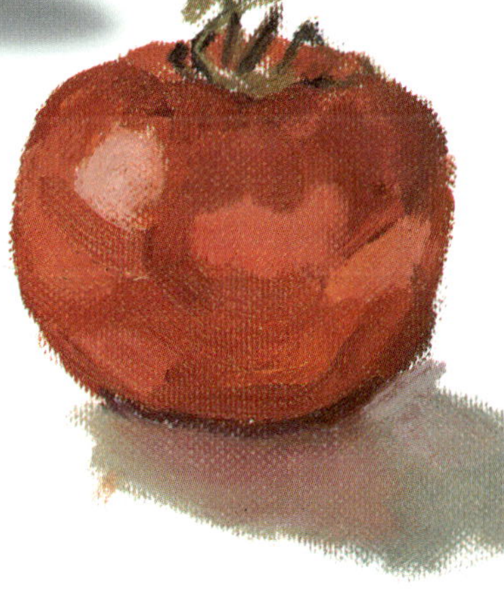

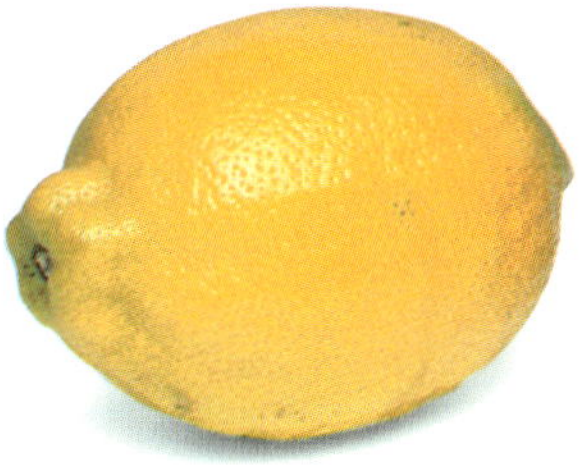

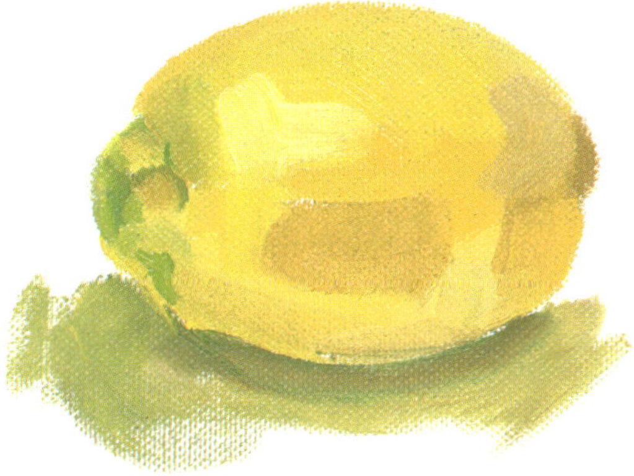

Greenish Lemon

For the lightest brushstrokes, yellow and white are mixed. The greenish tone is obtained by adding a little Permanent Green Light and white to the yellow. Ochre is used to darken the yellow. The shadow has been done with greenish hued brushstrokes, with Permanent Green Light, ochre, yellow, and a lot of white.

The Earth Colors

The earth colors, ochre, sienna, and umber, are the broken colors from our suggested palette. If we add yellow, red or crimson, greens or blues to any of them, their yellow, red, or blue qualities are modified.

Now let's go on to the actual mixing. The lightest ochre is obtained by adding yellow and white to ochre. The pinkest ochre is achieved by blending in a little red. For the darkest earth colors, mix sienna and umber. White is used for the lighter mixtures for shine and reflections. Note the tones that appear in the brushstrokes of the shadow.

REMEMBER...

- The range of warm colors transmits a feeling of warmth and yellow light.
- Painting with warm colors tends to create a pleasant, upbeat effect.

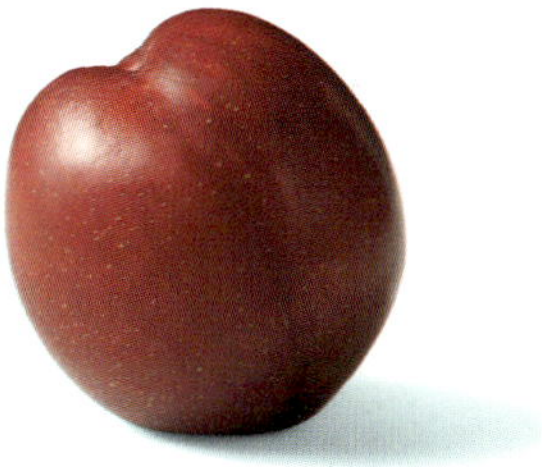

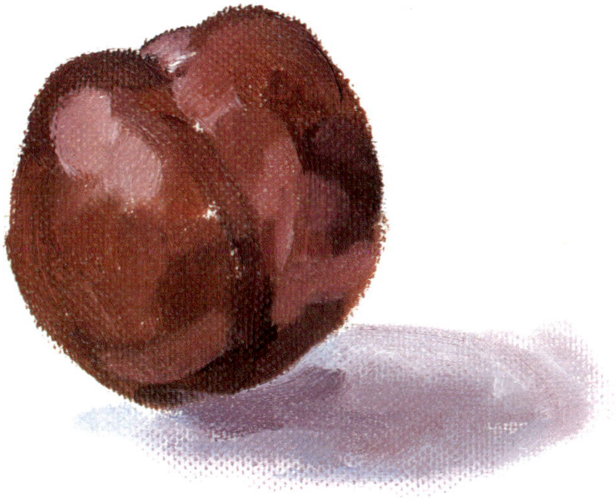

Darkening Crimson

The essential color for representing the cherry is crimson. This can be lightened by adding a little white and a little red. To darken it, a little ultramarine works wonders owing to its violet hue. The effect of volume is achieved by painting different tones. Note the purplish and maroon brushstrokes, with a lot of white, which give expression to the shadow the cherry casts.

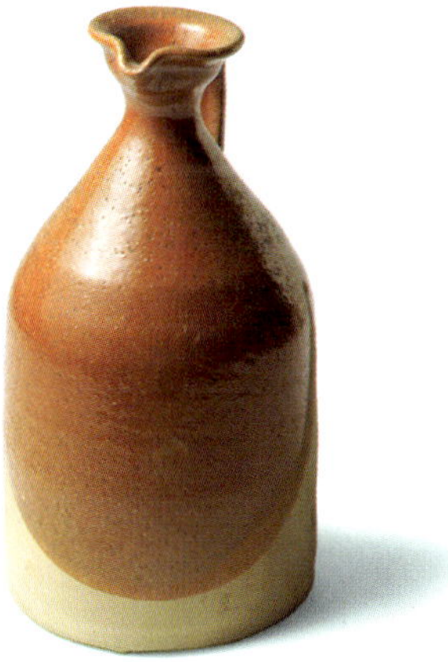

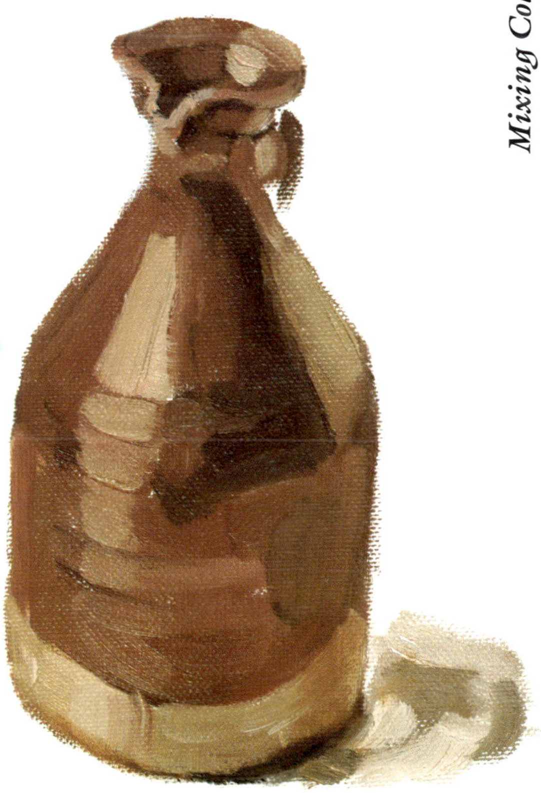

The Range of Cool Colors

Blue, above all, predominates among the cool colors. Painting with a range of cool colors gives the feeling of things far away, of atmosphere and distance. These are the colors of the horizon, the colors of dimly lit objects that tend to appear in bluish tones.

Creating Ranges

The following is a system for producing cool colors based on the palette we have been working with.

These scarves have been painted in Winsor Blue and ultramarine. White has been used for the lighter shades. For the violet hues, a little crimson has been added to the blue. The greens on the checkered scarf are obtained by adding yellow and Permanent Green Light.

The mixtures below are approximately those for each scarf. Each object is painted, blending and adjusting the mixtures, lightening them and darkening them as needed.

1. The basic color for scarf A is Winsor Blue tinged with a drop of yellow. In order to obtain more tones, darken with the tiniest amount of ultramarine or lighten with a little white.

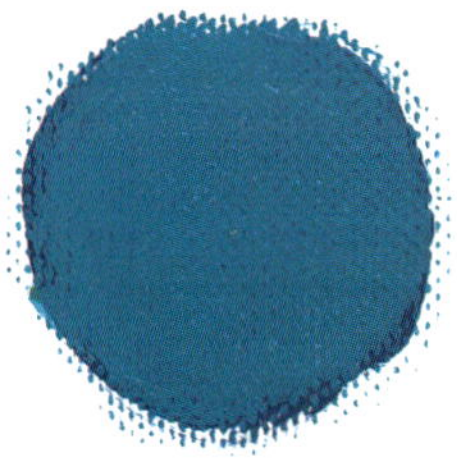

2. This is the light color of scarf B. There is a lot of Winsor Blue, a touch of ultramarine and yellow, and quite a lot of white.

3. Of all the blues, that of scarf C is the most violet. Less Winsor Blue is mixed than ultramarine. A touch of crimson and quite a bit of white are then added.

4. For the lightest brushstrokes in D, a little yellow is added to the Winsor Blue and this mixture is lightened with a lot of white.

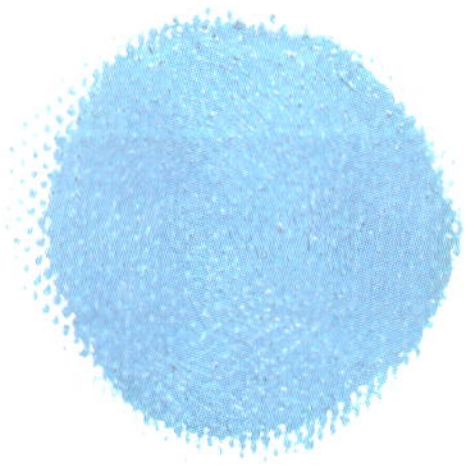

5. This medium tone of scarf D is a mixture of Winsor Blue and white.

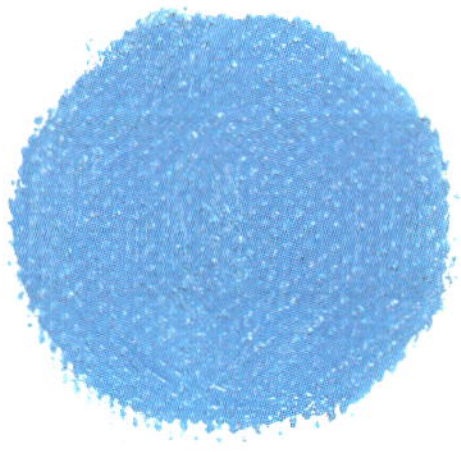

6. In this dark blue for E, ultramarine is mixed with a little crimson. This is then toned down with a little Chromium Oxide Green. Finally, a touch of white is added.

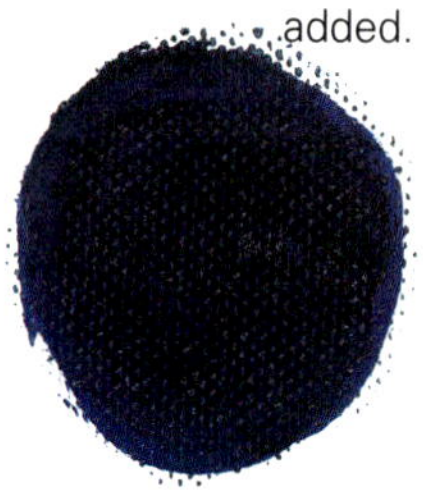

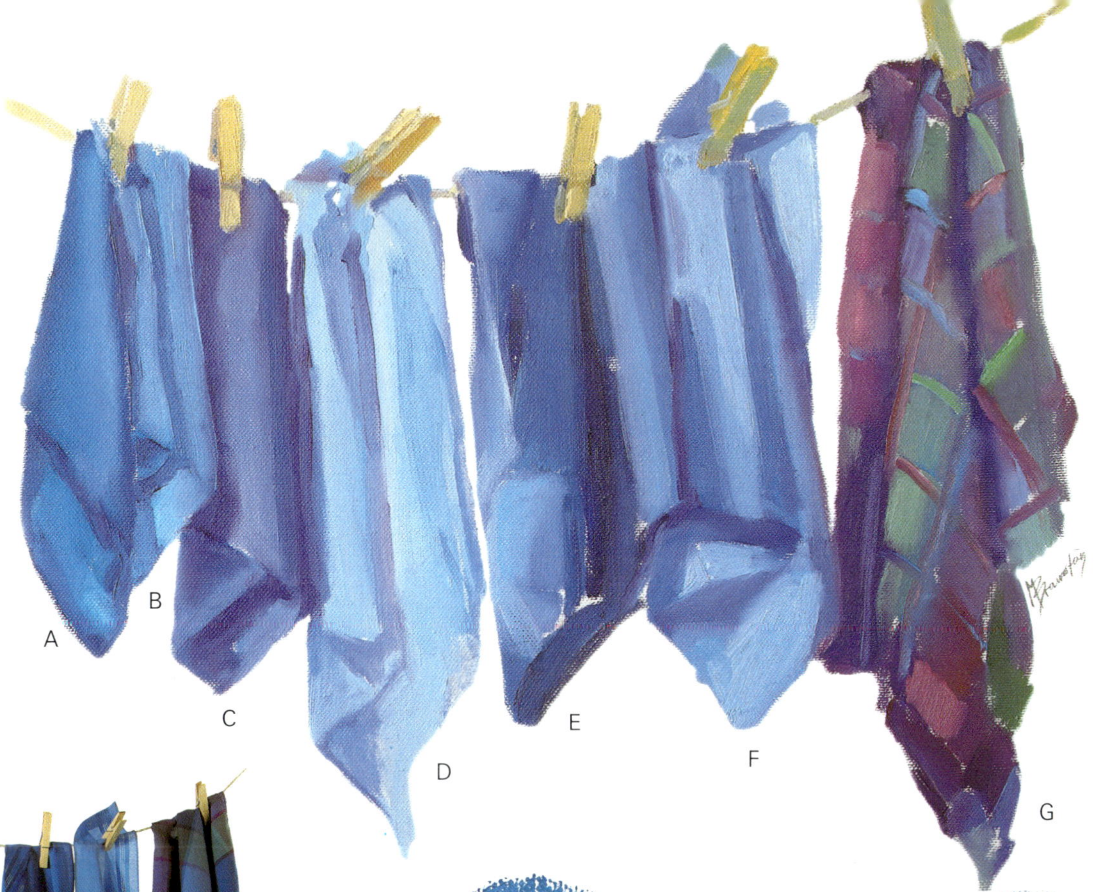

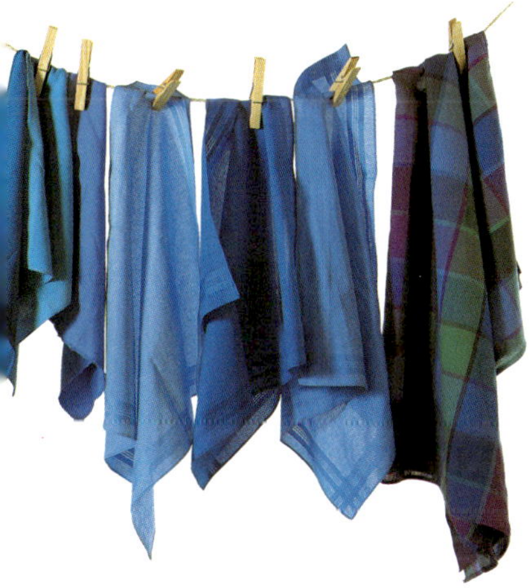

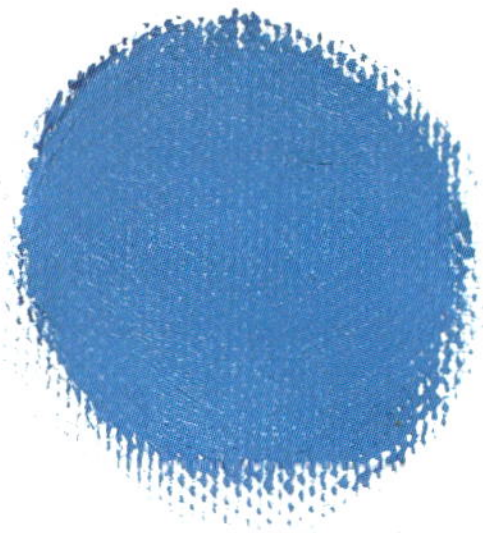

7. To obtain a blue like the one in E, a lot of Winsor Blue is mixed with little bit of ultramarine. A touch of crimson is added to the resulting mixture, and then a lot of white is blended in.

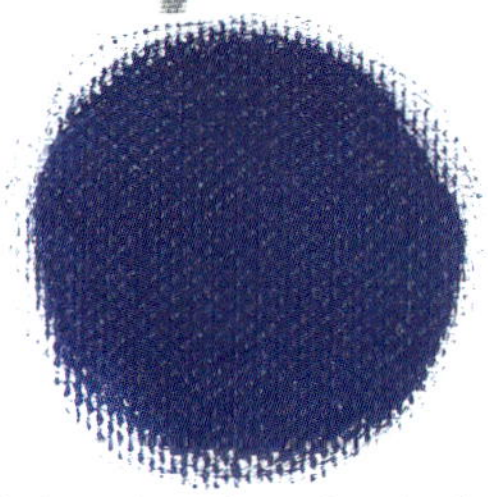

8. The darkest brushstrokes in F are violet colored. To a 50% mixture of Winsor Blue and ultramarine a tiny amount of crimson is added. The tone is then lightened with a little white.

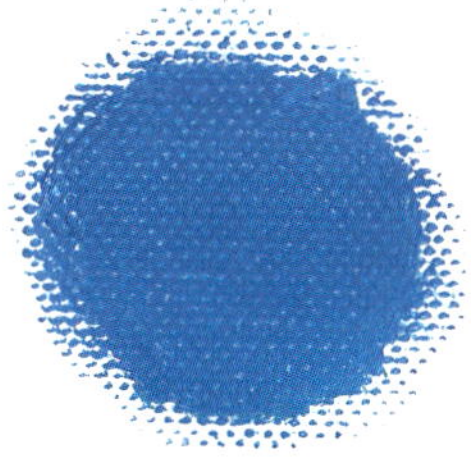

9. The medium tones of F are achieved with ultramarine, slightly lightened with some Winsor Blue and deepened somewhat using crimson. The right shade is obtained with a touch of white.

10. The green in scarf G is a mixture of Winsor Blue and yellow to which white has been added. To increase the green hue, a touch of Permanent Green Light can be added.

11. The crimson-violet in G is a mixture of a lot of crimson with some ultramarine and quite a bit of white.

12. Another pale purple for G. Crimson and a small amount of ultramarine are mixed, and then white is added.

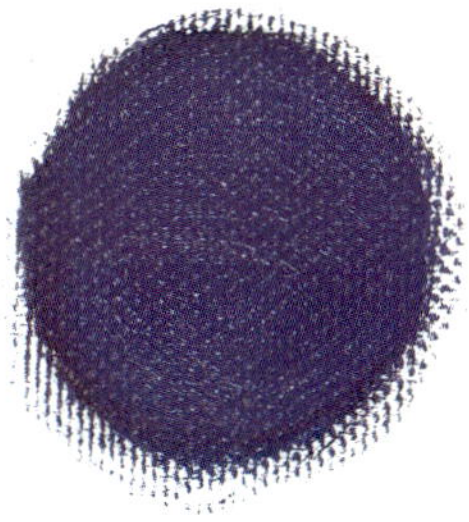

REMEMBER...

- Blue, above all, predominates in cool colors.
- The overall hue of a piece of work done in cool colors is blue.

The Range of Neutral Colors

A neutral or broken color is obtained by mixing two complementary colors in unequal proportions, lightening it, if necessary, with white. All the neutral colors present a definite grayish hue. They are not clearly defined colors. Together, they make up the range of broken colors.

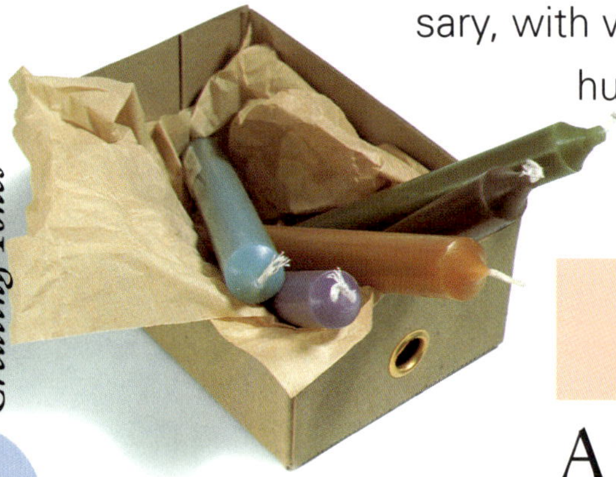

A box of candles. Model and painting.

The Attractive Neutral Colors

A neutral color always contains a quantity of each of the three primary colors. For this reason, it always has a muddy, grayish appearance. Every broken color has its own hue (warm, cool, or neutral), depending on the colors used to create it. This box of candles provides an opportunity to prepare a small range of neutral colors. Some are tones of the earth colors: ochre, sienna, and umber. Others, however, are obtained by mixing complementary colors. By trying out these mixtures you will discover the wealth of rich tones that can be achieved and the harmonies that can be established using these broken colors, creating contrasts that are both subtle and beautiful.

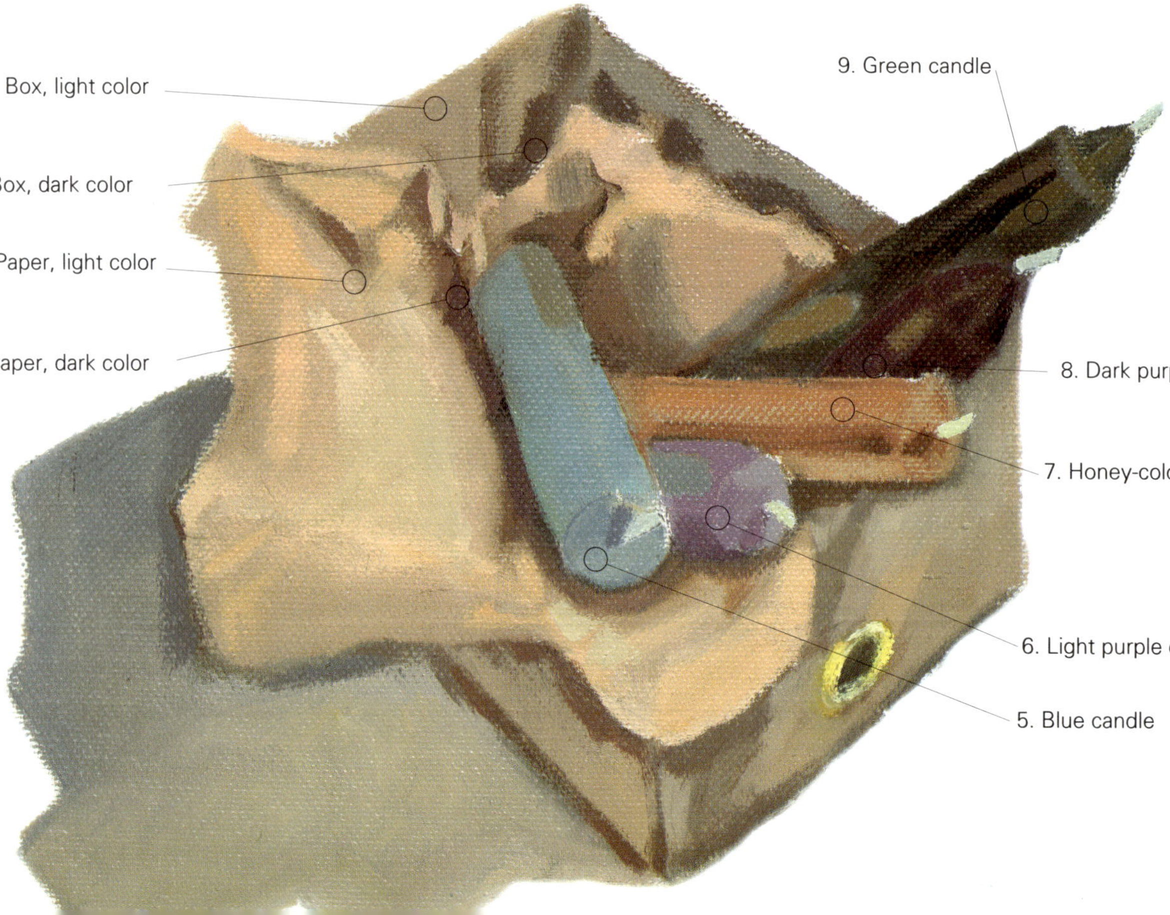

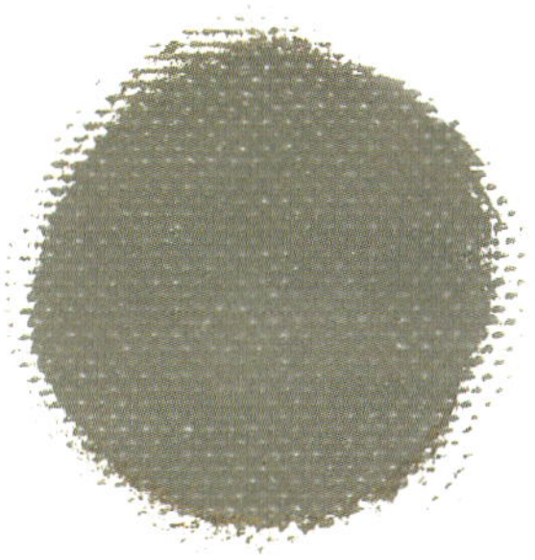

1. The same colors as in 2 but with a greater amount of white.

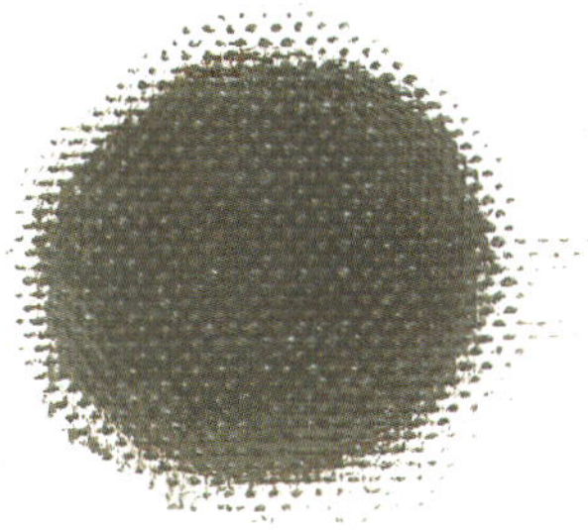

2. This gray is obtained by toning burnt umber with a little ultramarine and adding white.

3. Here the same colors as in 4 are used. The shade is grayer and lighter, because more white is used.

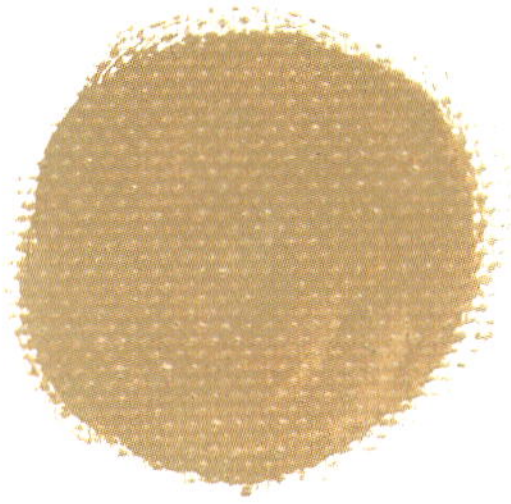

4. A mixture of yellow, vermilion, and ochre in equal amounts. White is added.

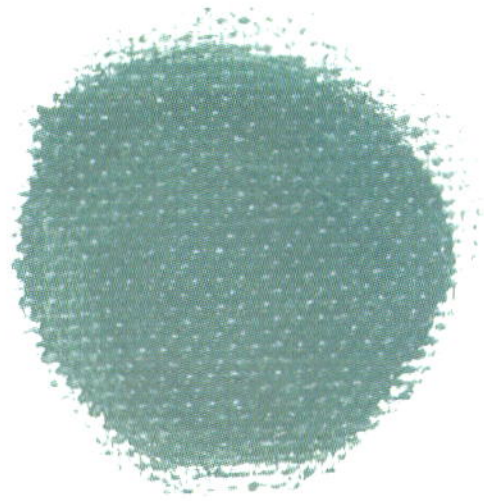

5. This grayish blue is obtained by mixing Winsor Blue with a little umber, adding white as required.

6. To tertiary violet (1 part crimson with 3 parts Winsor Blue) a touch of umber is added. Finally, the tone is lightened with quite a bit of white.

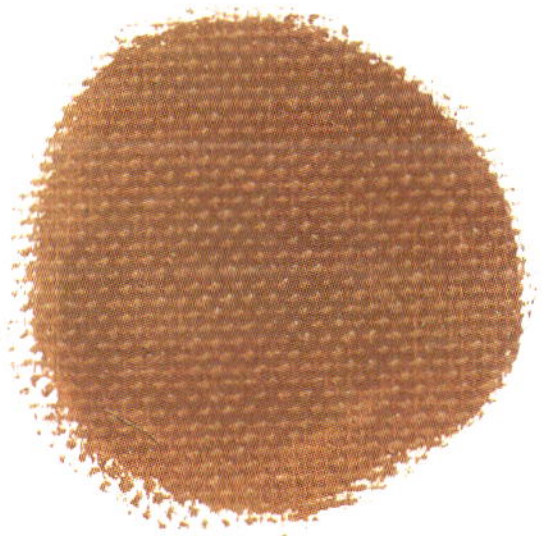

7. A nice honey color from sienna lightened with ochre and white.

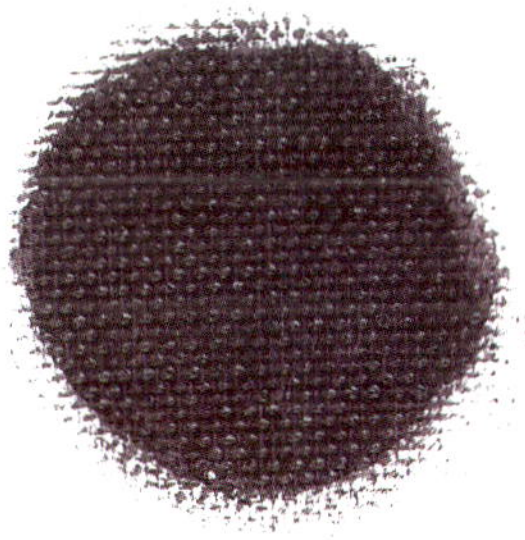

8. This mixture is also based on a violet as in 6, i.e. crimson, Winsor Blue, and little umber. This mixture is toned with a touch of white.

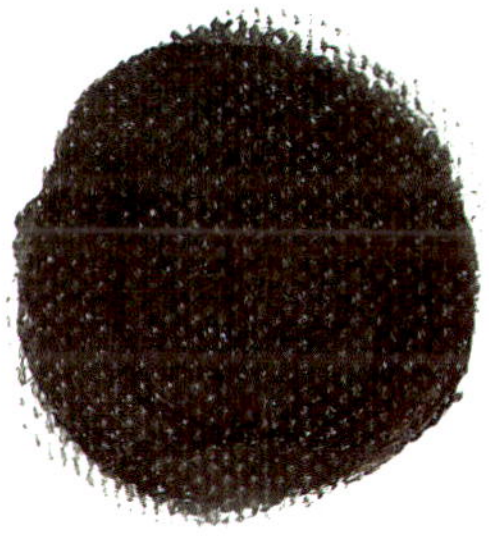

9. A muddy green obtained by mixing yellow, crimson, and Winsor Blue. Adjust accordingly, using mostly yellow, a little less blue, and less crimson than blue.

REMEMBER...

- To obtain broken colors with hues and shades, complementary colors are mixed in unequal proportions and white is added when required.
- Painting with a range of neutral colors gives a rich sense of hue and harmony.
- Broken colors can be graded. In the shadow cast by the box, the gradations progress from blue-gray to an earthy gray.

Judging the Tone

Here is an exercise to help you understand what we mean by the phrase: judging the tone. Observe the object—a sugar bowl—lit from the left. This object can be painted in a range of grays, mixing just black and white.

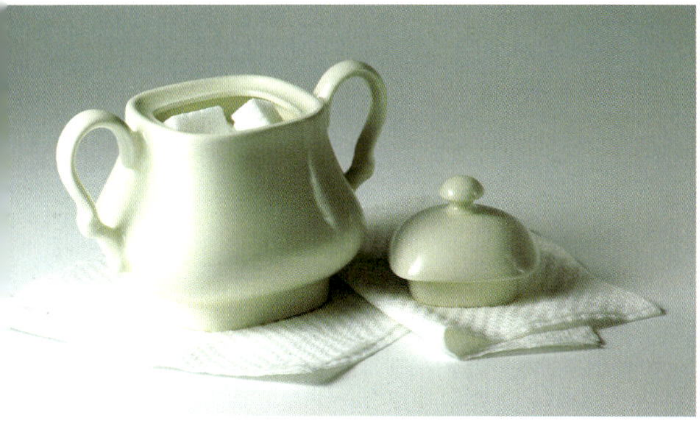

Model.

Sketching and Judging the Tone

Judging the tone is a method of measuring or grading the color tones. This exercise is carried out in opaque oils. As you observe the sugar bowl carefully you will begin to discern several shades of gray. The areas with the same shade are outlined. Then an order of tones is established. That is to say, the shades are graded, from the lightest (shine and reflections), to the darkest.

The sketch, lightly drawn in charcoal, describes the basic lines of the model on the canvas. The sketching of areas of tone indicates the edges of the most important areas of differing tones.

In order to obtain a good grading between different areas of shading, the brush (or finger) can be used to blend. Smooth blending will soften the harsh effect of excessive contrast between tones. See page 58 for more information about blending tones. Approach the painting of this sugar bowl by working from the lighter shades to the darker ones.

1. The charcoal sketch of the model is drawn onto the canvas using faint lines.

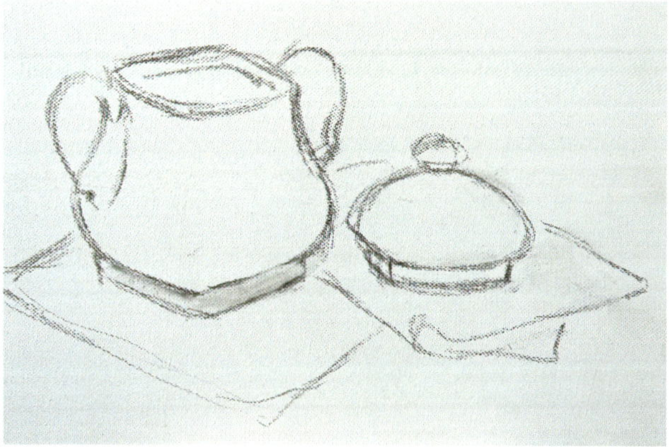

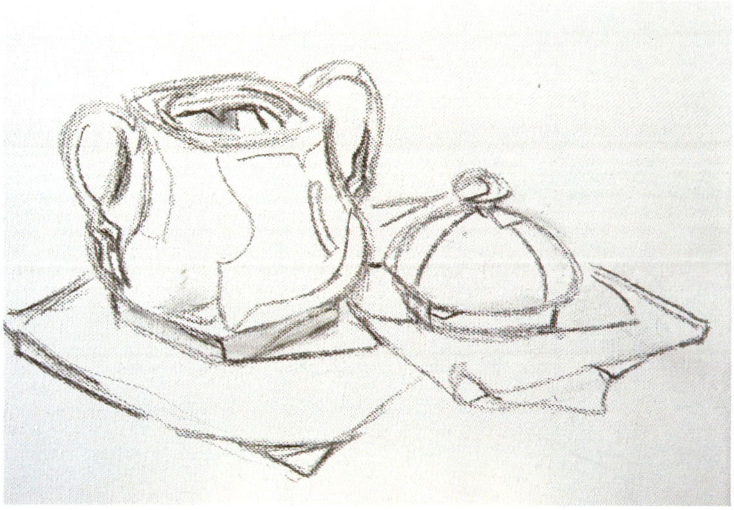

2. The outline of tonal areas is now drawn in order to make the delineation of tones clear. The fine lines separate areas of more similar shades.

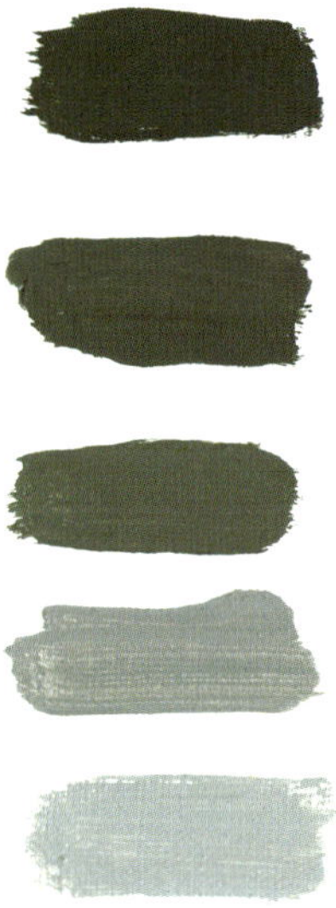

Color range obtained by mixing black and white.

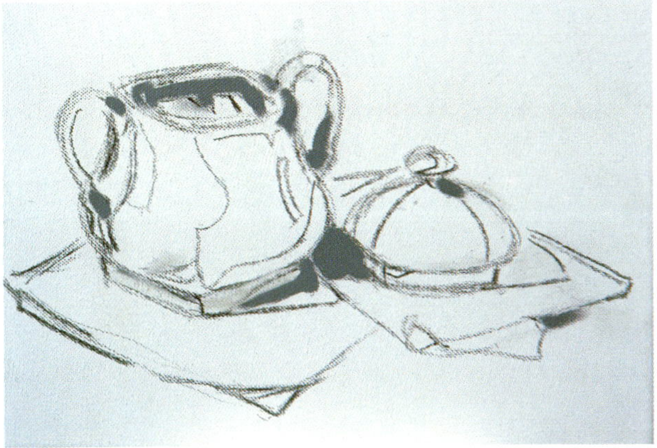

3. The darkest shades of the subject are painted in dark gray.

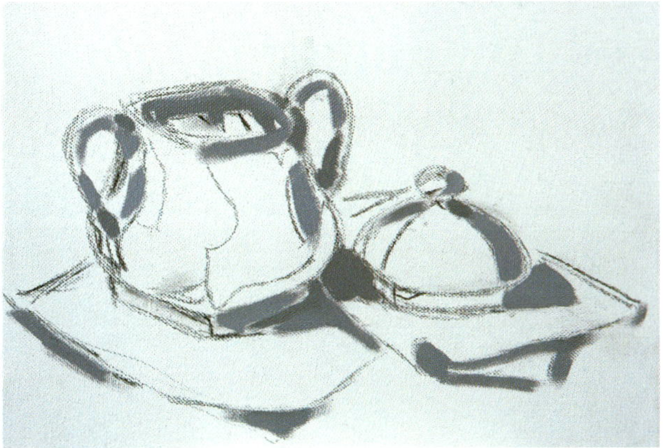

4. The next darkest areas are painted in a slightly lighter gray.

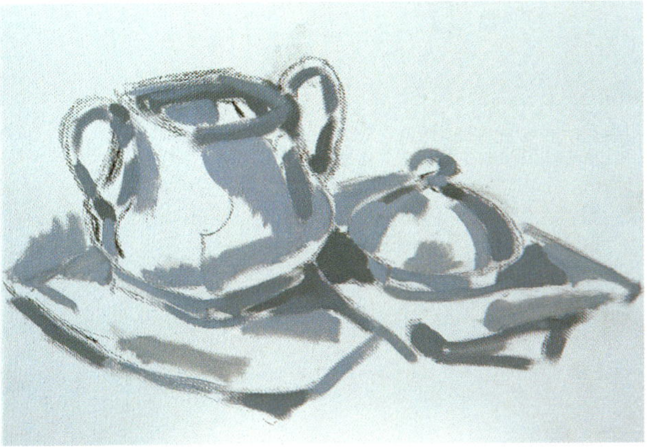

5. The next darkest areas progress to a still lighter gray.

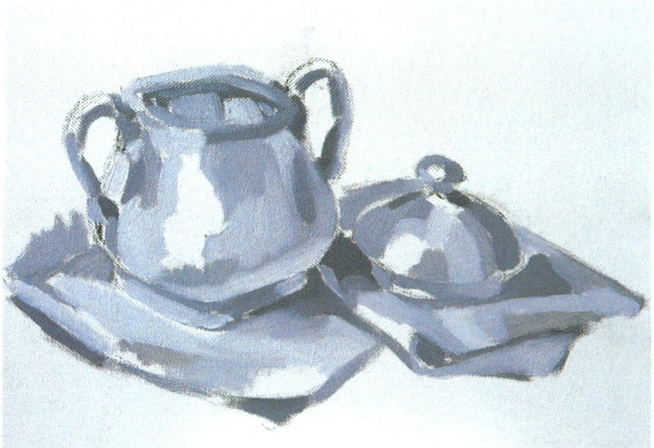

6. These areas have an ever lighter tone. Take care to preserve the lightest grays for areas of greatest shine and reflection, which will be dealt with in the next step.

REMEMBER...

- The sketch is useful for positioning the subject and locating the major lines.
- The different tones can be suggested in the sketch using very faint lines.
- Painting is carried out by developing a range of tones.

7. Here we have the final step. The aim of this exercise was to discern and visually organize the varying tones necessary for the representation of the subject as it appears. At this point the work is finished.

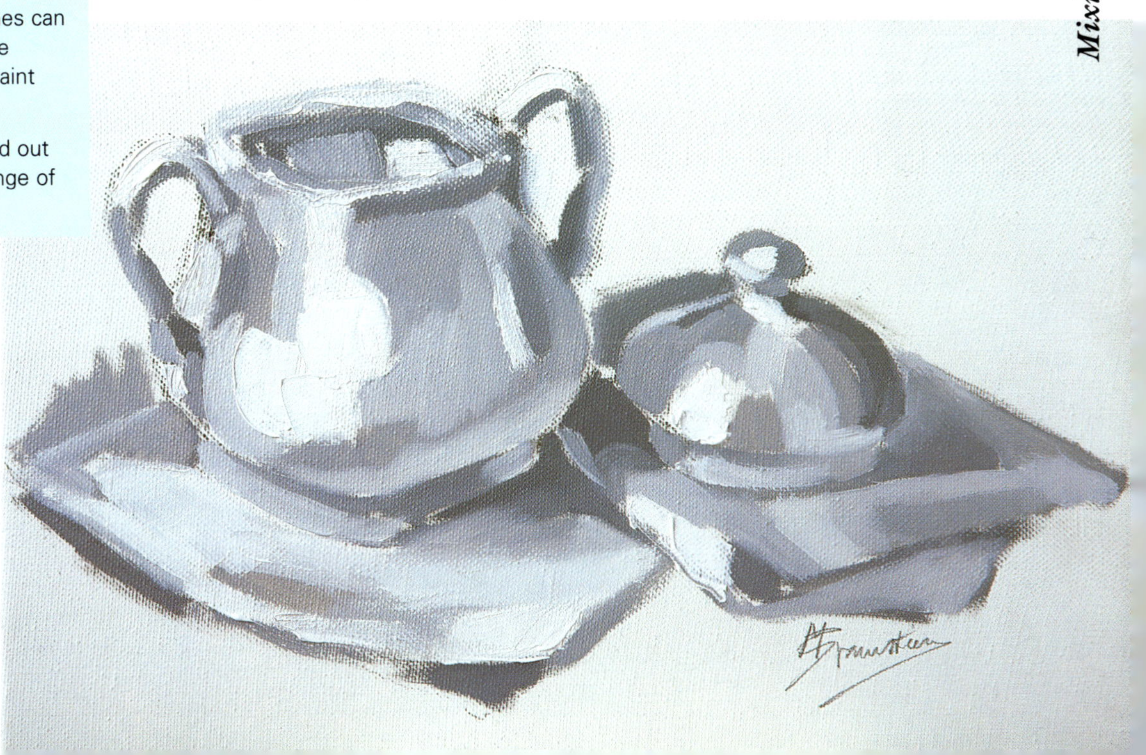

Using One Color with Turpentine

This exercise allows us to illustrate two important points: transparent grading and the advisability of a very diluted first layer.

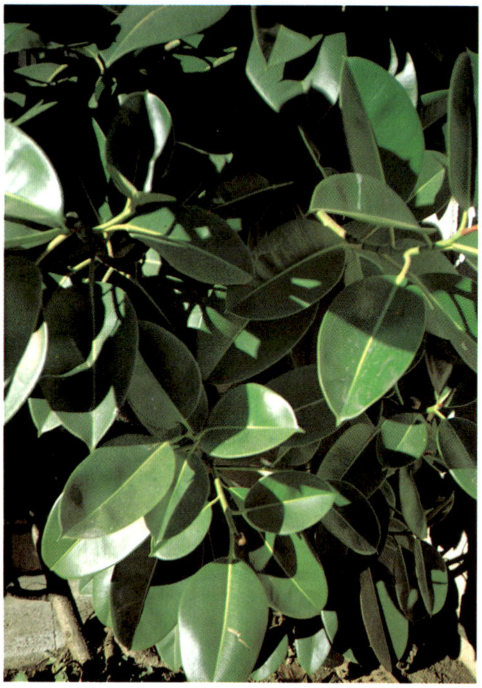

Grading a Color Transparently

You already know that a color can be graded by adding turpentine or linseed oil. Here, a range of transparent tones is produced on a fresh white canvas.

Take this rubber plant as a model. Chromium Oxide Green, progressively graded by diluting it with the addition of oil and turpentine, is a suitable color for this subject. The range of tones obtained will be transparent.

It is interesting to watch painting of this type progress through a series of different steps, starting off with unconnected patches and finishing up with a recognizable subject.

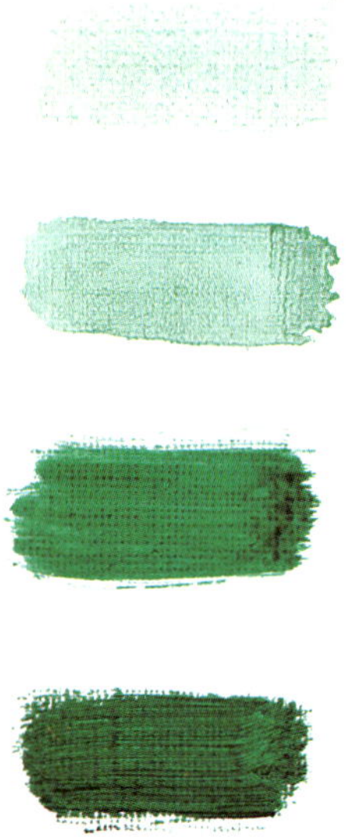

A range of several shades of Chromium Oxide Green. Each of the different tones has been obtained by thinning the paint and adding more and more of the oil and turpentine mixture each time. As the density diminishes, the color being painted appears lighter and more transparent.

REMEMBER...

- A transparent range of tones can be obtained for any color by diluting it with a solution of oil and turpentine, thus reducing its density.
- A first layer on a fresh canvas, carried out by grading a single color transparently, provides a good base and guide, once dry, for continuing to paint another layer during a second session.

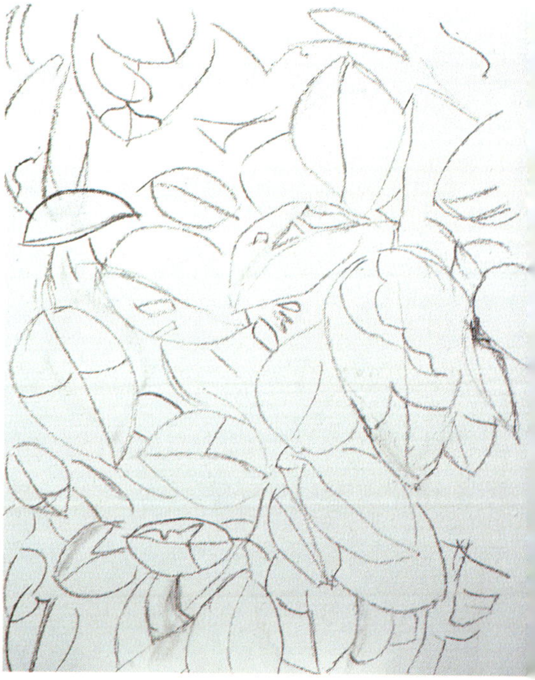

1. The sketch of the areas of different tones is drawn very lightly in charcoal.

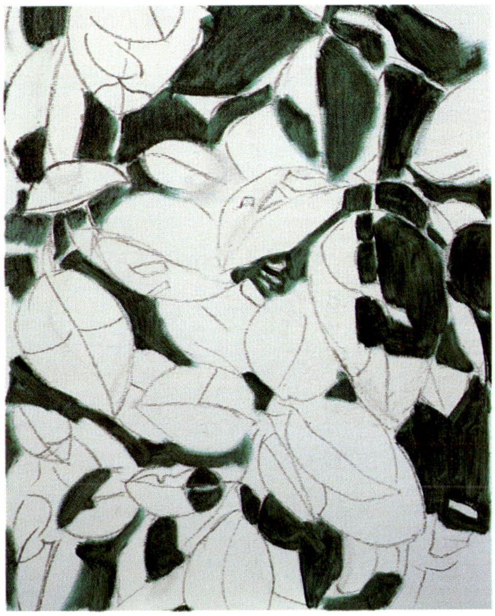

2. Begin to paint in Chromium Oxide Green that has been only slightly diluted so that the brush will slide easily across the canvas. This is the densest paint and, with it, the darkest leaves and shadows are filled in.

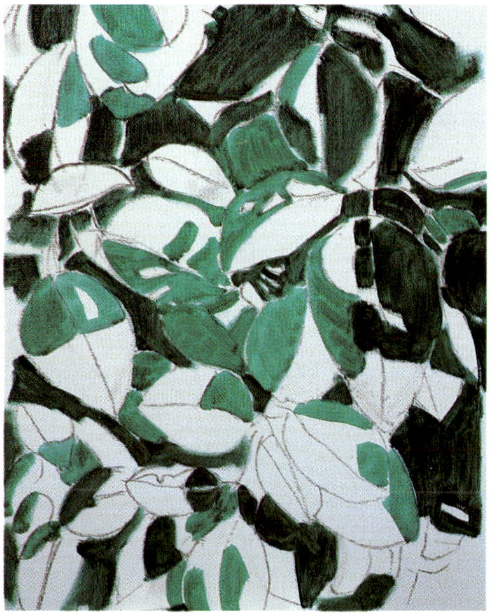

3. Following the same process, the work now continues but with a thinner mixture of Chromium Oxide Green than in step 2.

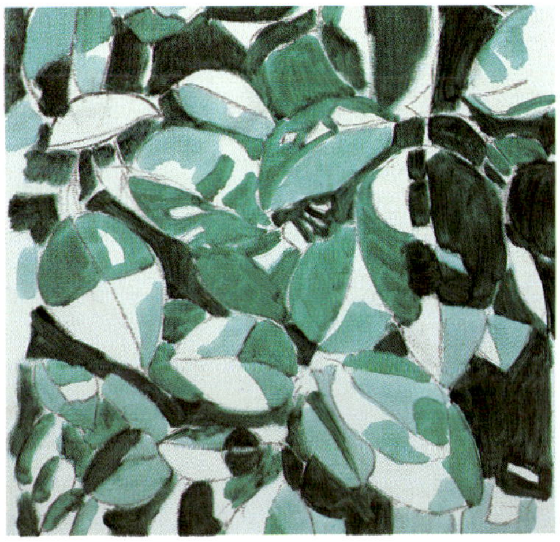

4. Using the same method the next set of tones are now done using a lighter Chromium Oxide Green than in step 3.

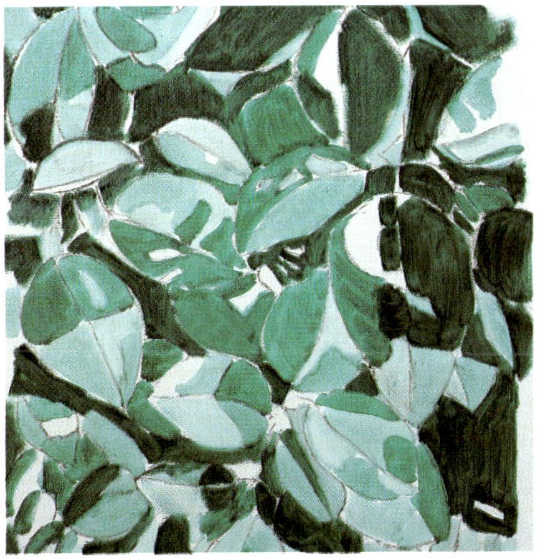

5. Now an even lighter shade is used. This is a very transparent tone. The areas of maximum light are left blank.

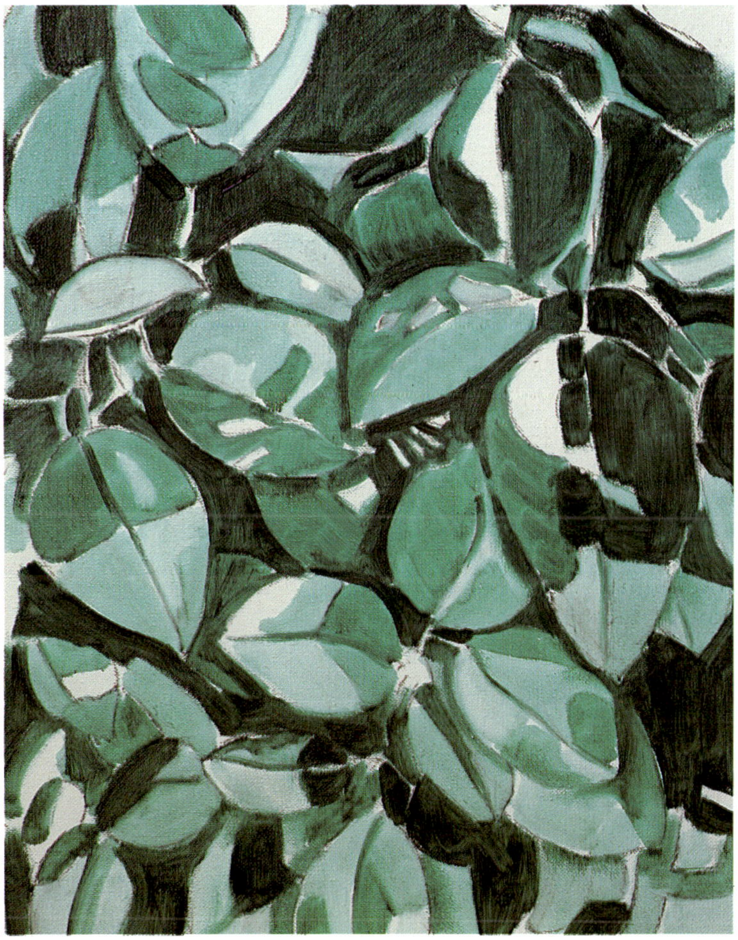

6. In this final step, we do any necessary finishing up of the shapes and do some outlining of the edges. Now we have a fine first layer for our painting. When painting in oils, a piece of work dries by oxidation with the air. The upper layers dry first. To avoid cracking, thick should be painted over thin. This means that the first layer, the first patches that you paint, should be painted in diluted form, as we have done. Once dry, a second layer can be painted over it, without any mixing of the two layers of paint. The final piece will then dry without cracking.

Choosing a Palette with Few Colors

The model suggests the palette of colors most suitable for painting it. Here is an example. A floral theme, such as these gerbera daisies, is a good model for beginning to paint. It can be done with few colors and with simple mixtures, while also being fairly simple to draw. It is a good subject for exploring the use of the palette knife as a painting tool.

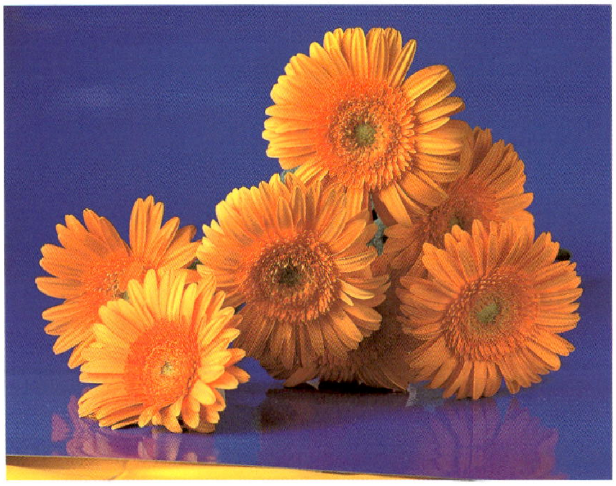

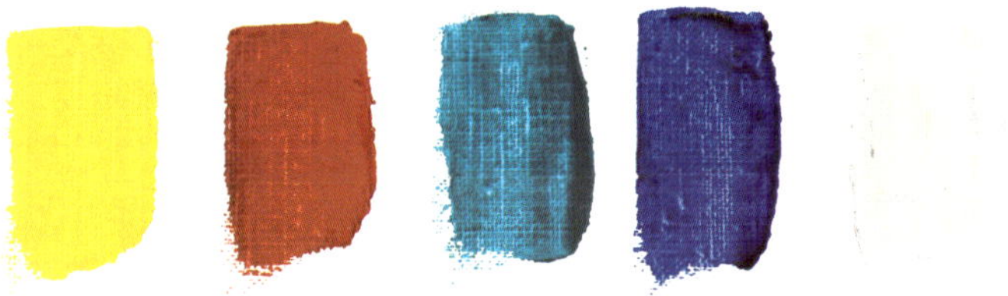

Colors that will be used in the mixture, from left to right: yellow, vermilion, Winsor Blue, ultramarine, and white.

The Subject and the Palette

Choosing the colors you are going to paint with depends on the subject used as a model. For these flowers, it is evident that we have to develop two ranges, one of oranges and one of blues.

If we remember that tertiary orange is obtained with yellow and red, for the range of oranges we can place the yellow and vermilion on the palette. For the range of blues, we have ultramarine and Winsor Blue at our disposal. And finally, white will allow us to obtain lighter shades.

By using a palette knife to paint we will try to represent the essence of the whole, rather than painting each petal of every flower.

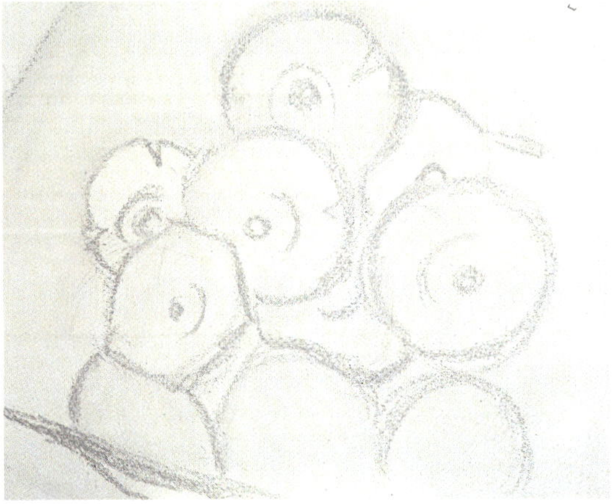

1. All the flowers are sketched generally and lightly, using charcoal.

REMEMBER...

- The subject chosen as a model will suggest the colors you will need for mixing.
- The reflections on the table's blue surface will require mixing yellow, red, and blue. These are the only broken colors you will need to represent this image.

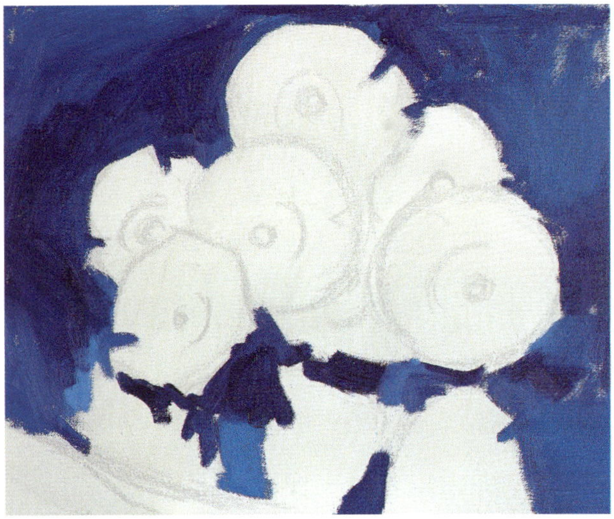

2. Now, with a paintbrush and slightly diluting the colors, the background is filled in using a mixture of blues. In the lightest shades, there is more Winsor Blue. In the darkest tones there is a good deal of ultramarine.

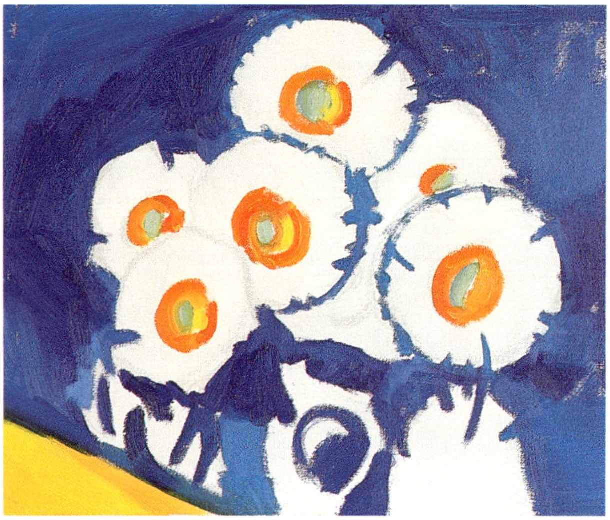

3. The centers of the flowers are painted using red and deep orange. Note the color in the center. It is a very pale green, mixed from yellow and a little Winsor Blue, adding white as necessary.

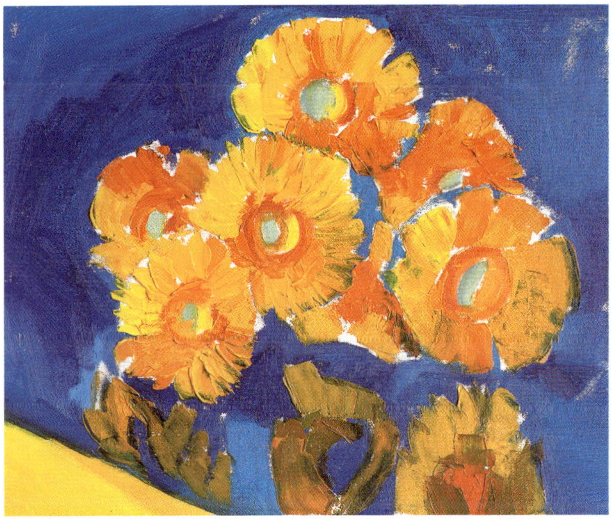

4. Now, with the palette knife, boldly lay onto the surface of the canvas the range of oranges that represent the petals. These are mixtures of yellow and vermilion. Above all, everything should not be painted in the same shade of orange. Observe and try to vary the different shades and tones. The palette knife is used in a pressing, linear motion, following the direction of the petals.

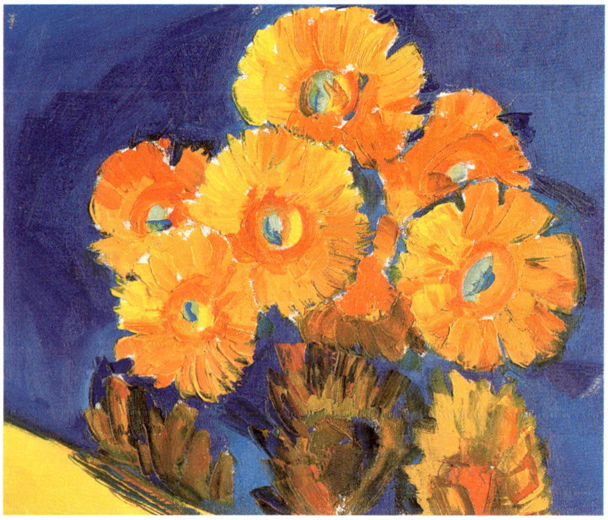

5. In this step, the tones and contrasts have been enriched. Continue with the palette knife to obtain more shades of orange. Add more blue tones with the paintbrush.

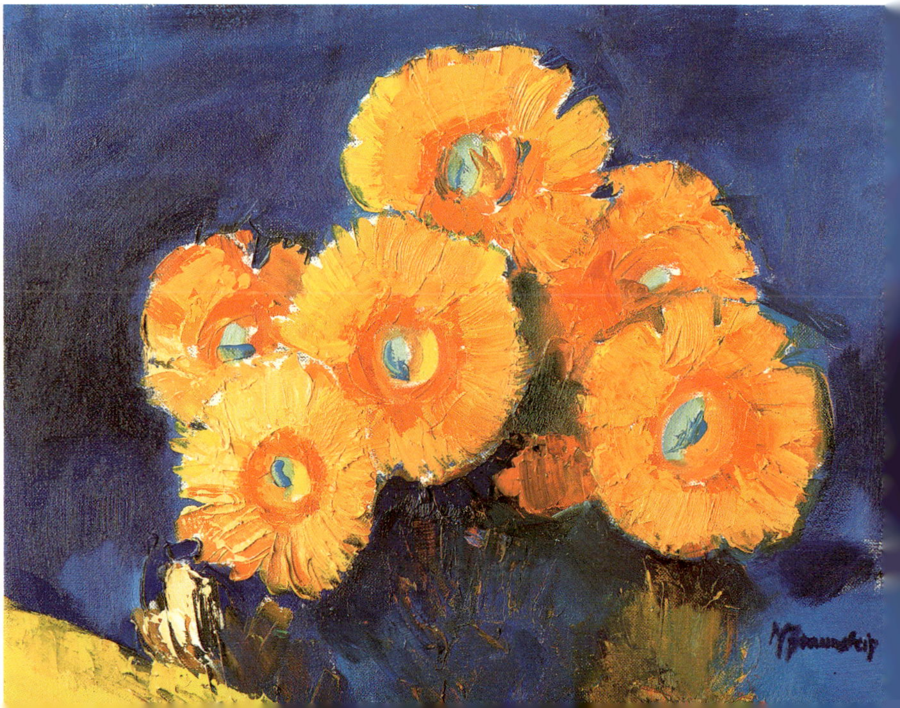

6. In the final step we have to take stock of the work done so far. This is the time to correct and adjust. Darken the background with a little more ultramarine so the flowers stand out and show greater depth. But since the intense ultramarine reflections on the blue background reduced the impact of the flowers, they have been toned down with a little Winsor Blue. Now the orange daisies are the clear focal point.

Painting in Patches

This is a color exercise in which the drawing is a secondary element. The work will be done in layers over several work sessions. The color of the first layer on the fresh canvas should be diluted to avoid cracking. For a piece done in layers, the first layer is only applied as an undercoat to build a foundation for the second layer.

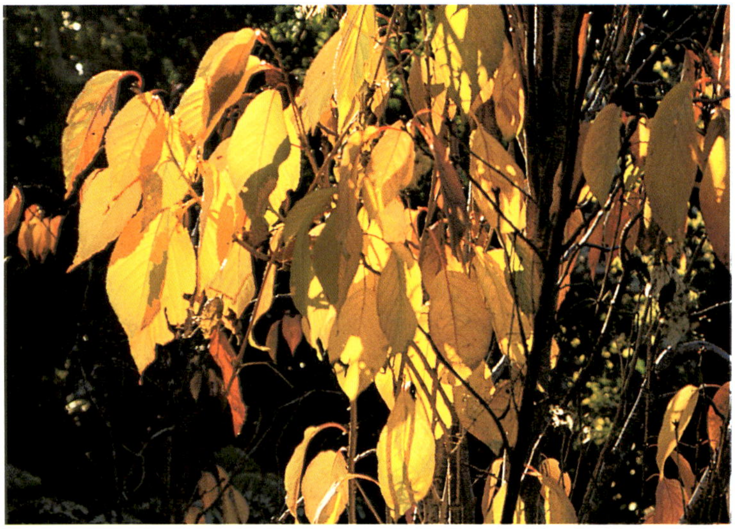

Patches

For this exercise we will begin by painting the whole of the support surface in one color only, in this case a thinned down red. Afterward, before it dries, enough paint is removed using a cotton rag wrapped around your finger to sketch out by removal of color the principal shapes of the subject. This is another way of outlining or blocking in different areas as you prepare them for the varying tones of graded colors.

All the colors of our palette will be used in the mixtures for this exercise.

1. In order to gain a clear understanding of the subject, it is a good idea to sketch out the composition, in pencil for example, on a separate piece of paper.

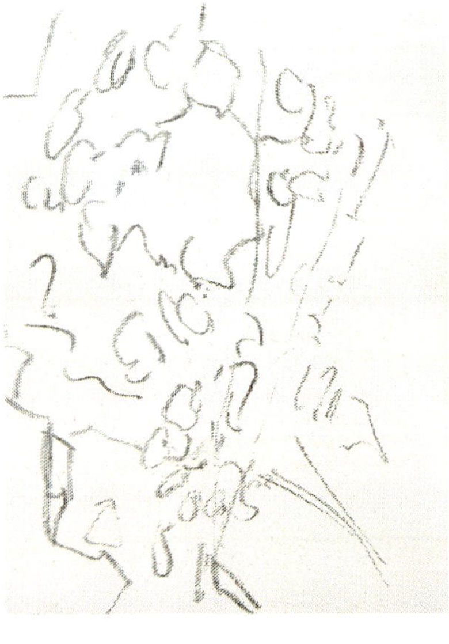

2. Now cover the whole of the canvas with a diluted deep red (crimson and vermilion in equal parts).

3. With the help of a cotton rag remove the wet red paint from the necessary areas, beginning to block in or suggest your shapes and forms.

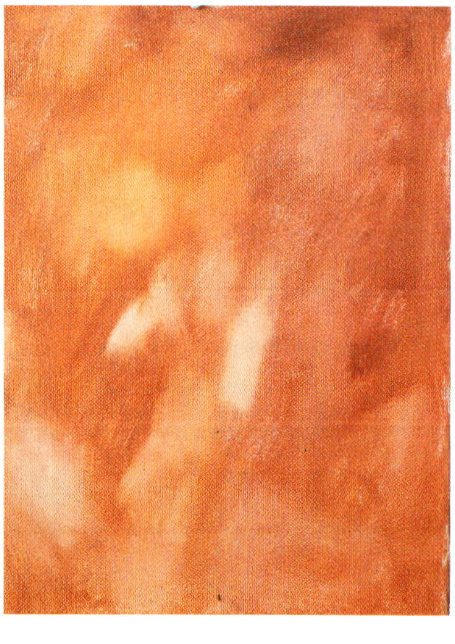

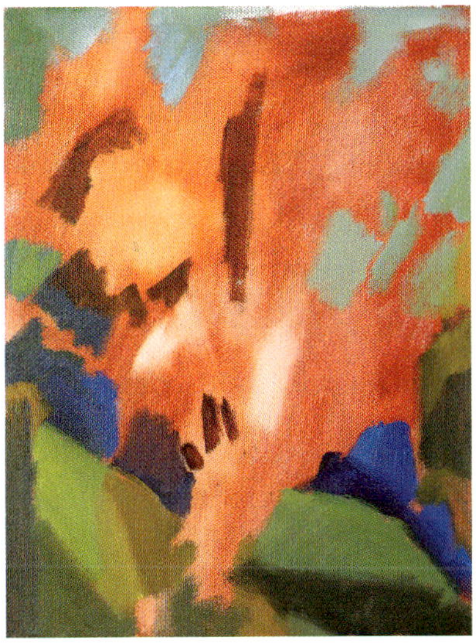

4. The main areas of the bush can now be filled in using soft colors.

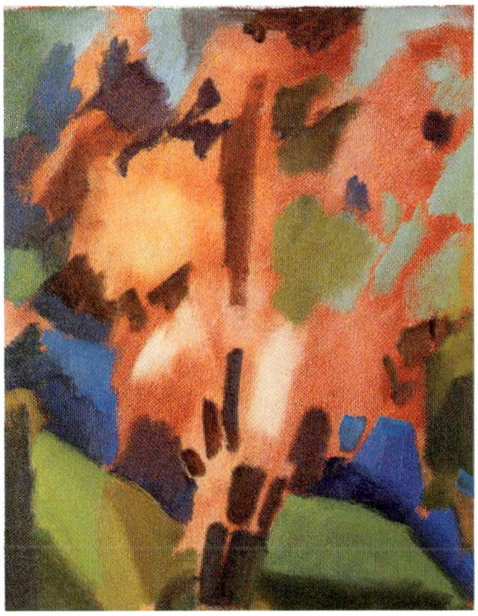

5. Continue to develop a rich background of the painting with different colored tones.

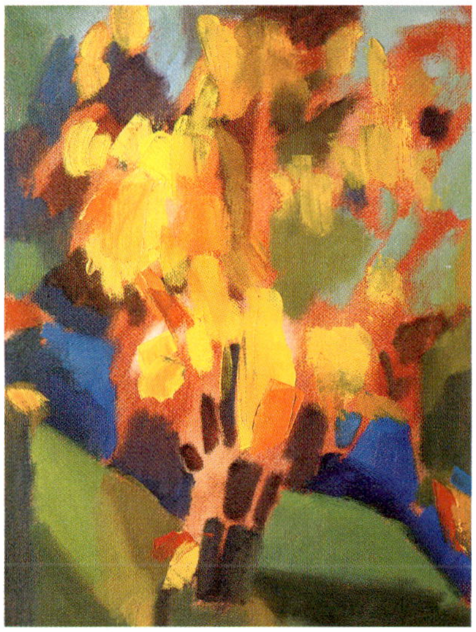

6. Now the warmer colors are painted in. The lighter areas are patched with mixtures consisting of much yellow and a little vermilion. The mixtures are toned down and darkened with a little ochre.

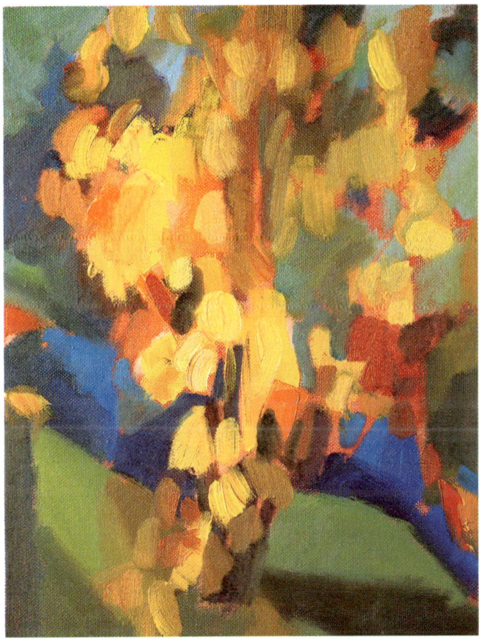

7. Continue enriching the painting with golden yellows, ruddy hues, and even greens. Now we will allow it to dry.

8. At this final stage it is time to step back and assess what may be needed to provide some finishing touches. When painting in patches, it is important to maintain a balance between abstraction and the representation of your subject. It is time to retouch and correct everything that helps to make the painting more understandable. Painting in opaque oils allows you to cover and completely block out any area of dry paint as you adjust your forms or make any desired corrections.

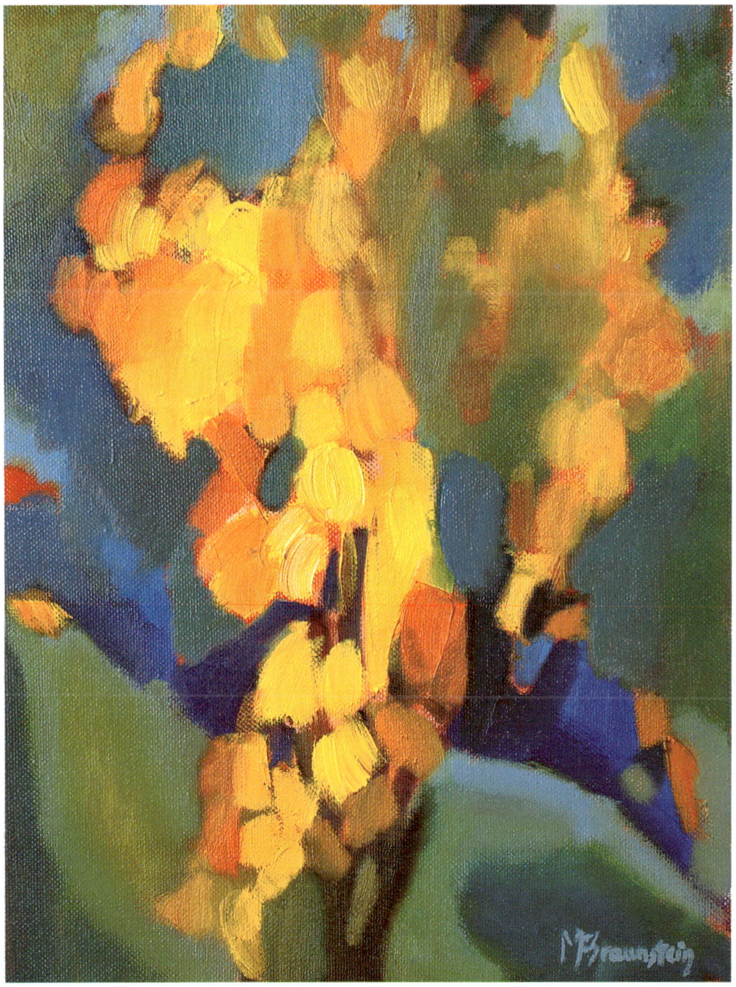

Painting a Seascape in Cool Colors

Since sea and sky usually dominate a seascape, you will most frequently be working with large areas of blues.

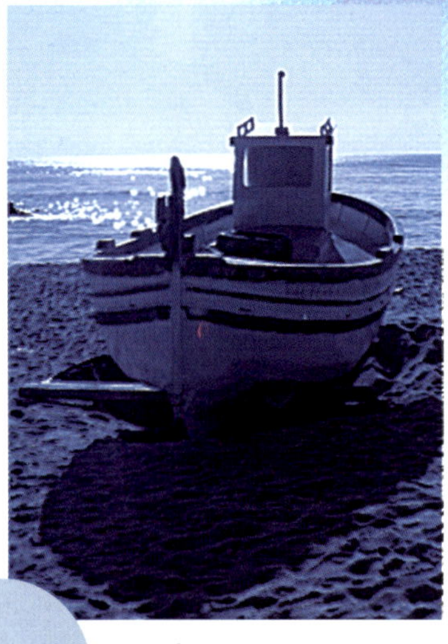

Seascape with boat.

The Dominant Color

The seascape used as our subject is heavily weighted with blue, created in this photograph by adding a blue filter. This "trick of the trade" brings up an important point: the artist's interpretation of the subject, interpreting, modifying, exaggerating its features, plays a dominant role in the making of art. In this exercise, even if the true shades of light and dark in the original subject do not correspond to the resulting painting, an exquisite composition using a cool range of clean and broken colors has been created.

These are the colors that are going to be used in the mixtures for painting this seascape. We shall use ochre, Winsor Blue, ultramarine, and white.

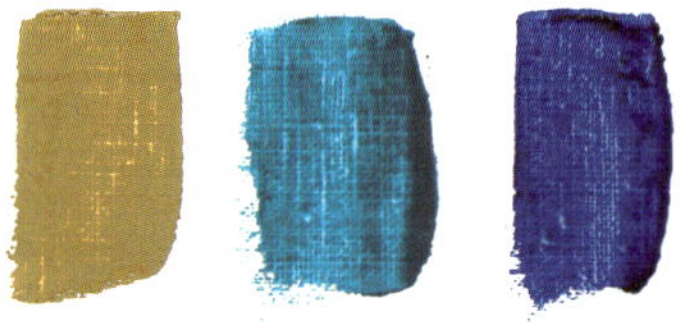

1. The sketch is drawn faintly in charcoal. Draw the boat slightly to the left of the center as it makes a composition visually more interesting to be slightly off balance. There are two important lines in relation to the boat. One is the horizon, separating the sea and the sky in the far distance; the other is the line that marks the shoreline.

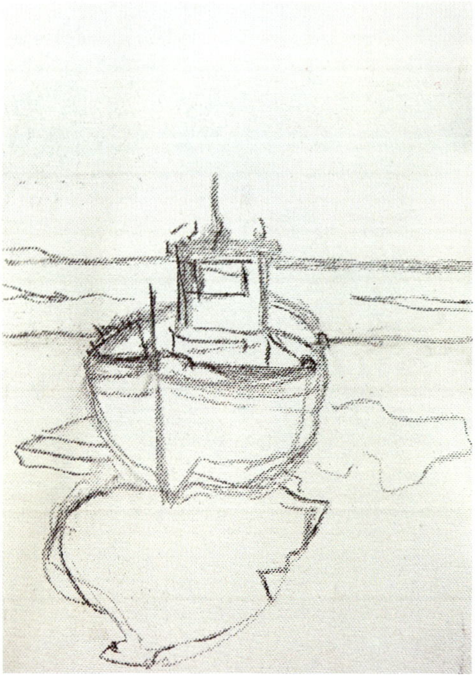

2. All the paint for this first layer will be diluted with oil and turpentine. The work will be done in three layers in the course of three work sessions. Here, only the two blues are used for the mixtures. The sky is a gradation with Winsor Blue. For the sea, Winsor is mixed with ultramarine. The shadows are painted with ultramarine. The boat is blocked in with Winsor Blue. A mixture of blues is used for the sand. Then it is left to dry.

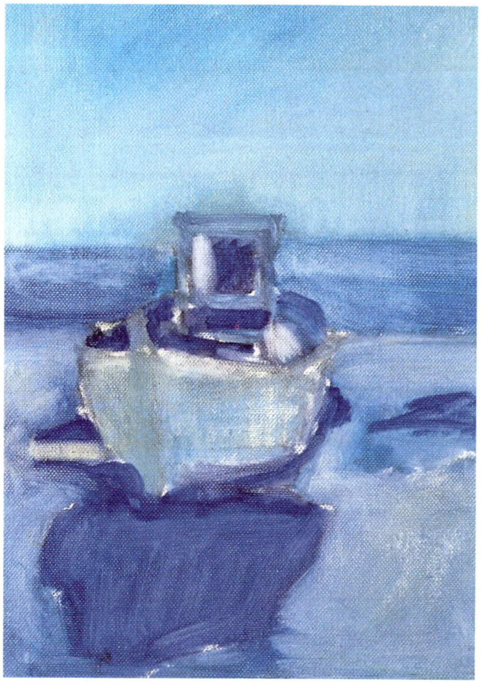

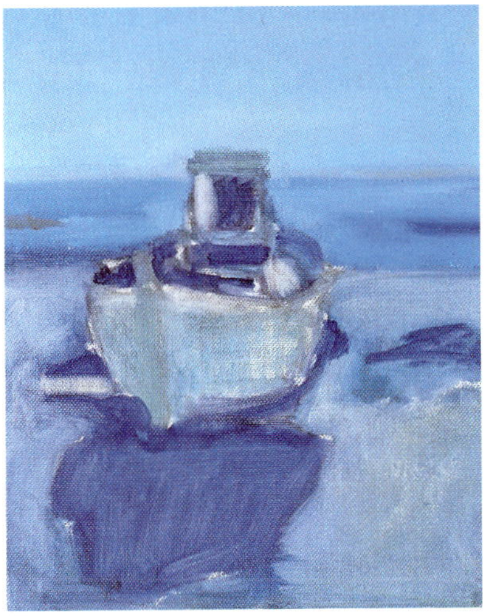

3. After allowing the first layer to dry, we start the second. The sky is filled in using more opaque paint, graded with white, a mixture with a lot of Winsor Blue and little ultramarine. For the sea, which is darker, the mixture contains more ultramarine than the sky.

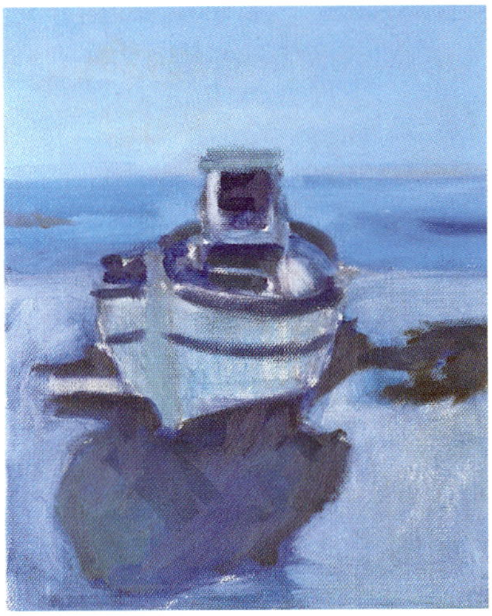

4. The dark contrasts of the boat and the sand in the foreground are painted with a mixture of ultramarine lightly toned with ochre.

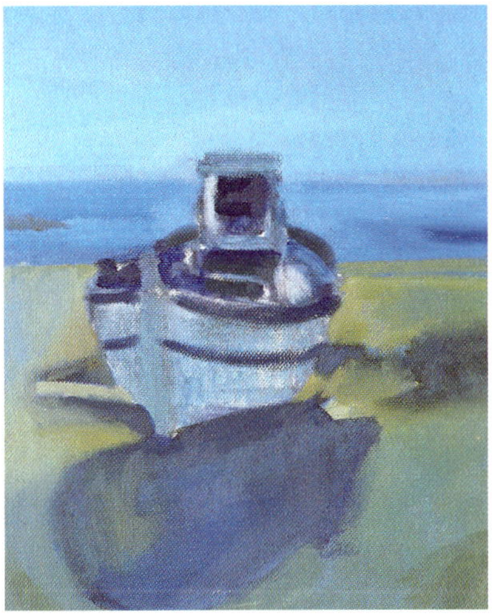

5. For painting the sand, a greenish range is mixed using ochre and the blues tinted with a lot of white.

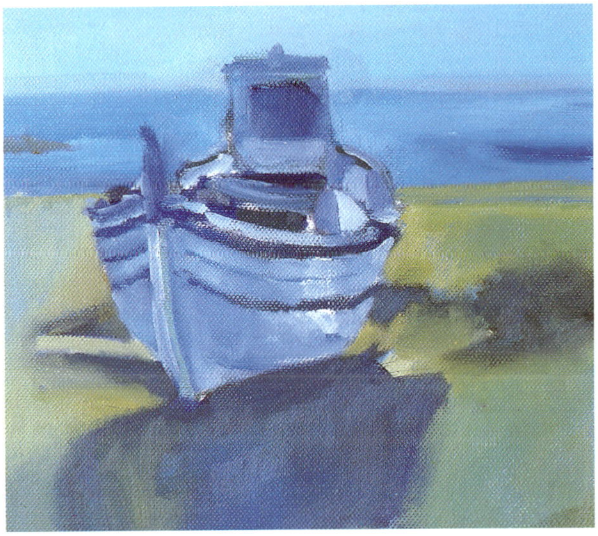

6. The boat is painted using the blues and a lot of white, creating a range of very light tones. The contrasts are kept between the light and dark. Then the piece is left to dry again.

REMEMBER...

- Working to obtain extensive ranges of colors is the secret behind achieving the rich hues of oil paint.
- When blue does not predominate a subject, the blues can be complemented with warm colors producing rich grays and creating shadows.

7. As you come up to finish you will note that two things can still be adjusted: the tones in the sand, and the degree of illumination of the boat. For the sand, a very transparent veil of Winsor Blue, quite diluted with oil and turpentine, is applied. The boat is painted over with a range of lighter blues, using more white. Dabs of white are used for the reflections.

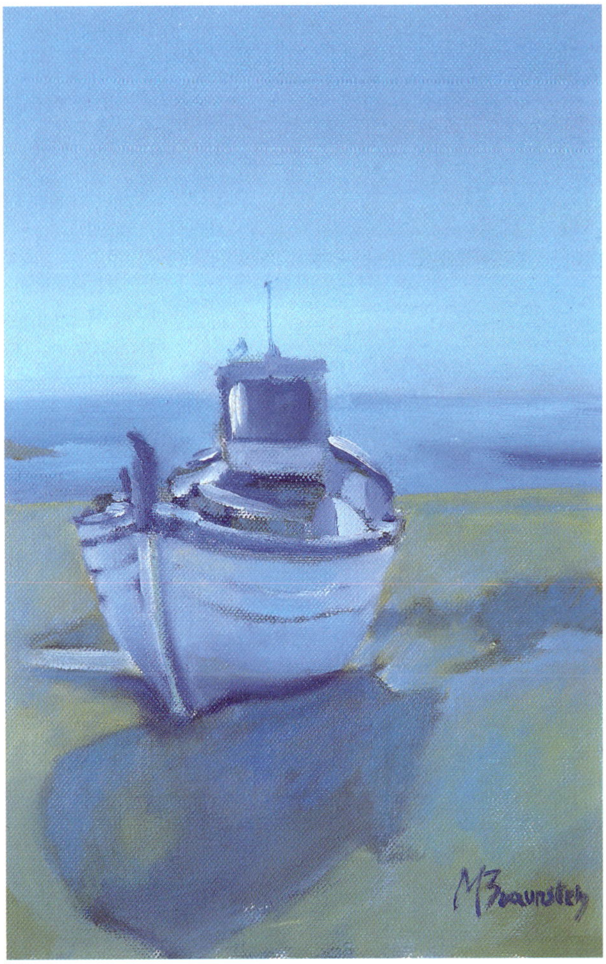

Painting a Landscape in Neutral Colors

A gray is the mixture, in different proportions, of the three primary colors; a mixture that can be lightened as required with white. Grays are negated, neutralized, or broken colors. An outdoor scene with little light, where a lot of zones are cast in shade, is ideal for painting in neutral colors.

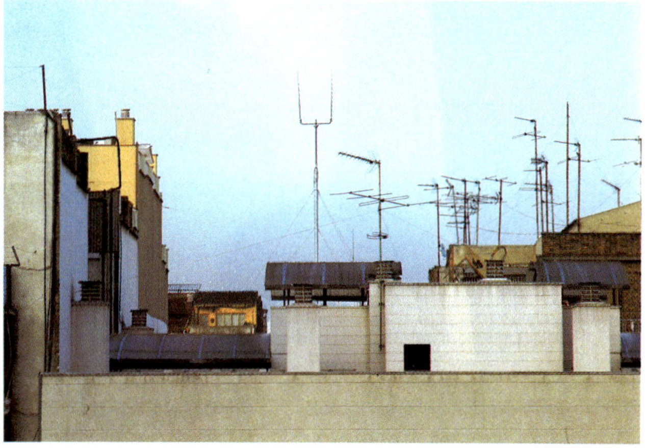

A Palette Suited to the Subject

For this urban landscape, ranges will have to be mixed in two color groups, one warm and the other cold. The warm neutral colors correspond to the parts of the buildings still lit by the last rays of the setting sun. The mixtures are created from the earth colors in our palette, lightened with yellow and white and darkened with blues. The cool neutral colors are used in the areas of shade. For the cool broken colors, the blues are mixed with either burnt umber or white.

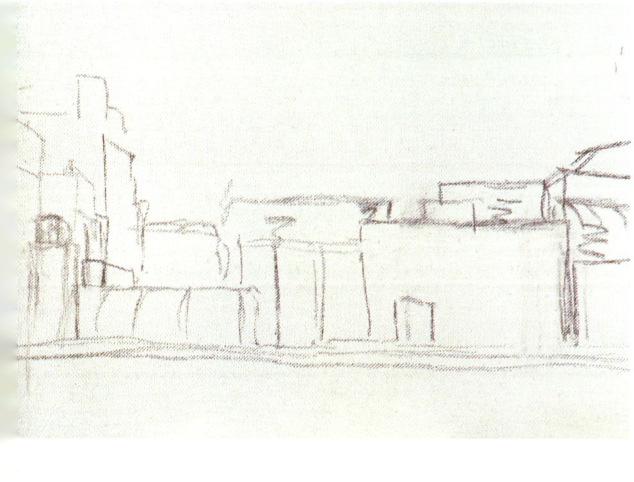

1. In the sketch, the dominant horizontal line is that of the skyline. Perspective is indicated in the lines of the buildings on the left. It is not necessary to do a perfect charcoal drawing in this townscape; it is only important to convey the general image of the block. The sketch needs only generally to resemble the model.

REMEMBER...

- The colors umber, ochre, and sienna are broken colors. Any mixture with them will produce neutral, broken colors.
- When a neutral color is composed of more warm colors than cool colors, it will have a warm cast or hue. Conversely, if blue predominates, it will acquire a cool hue.

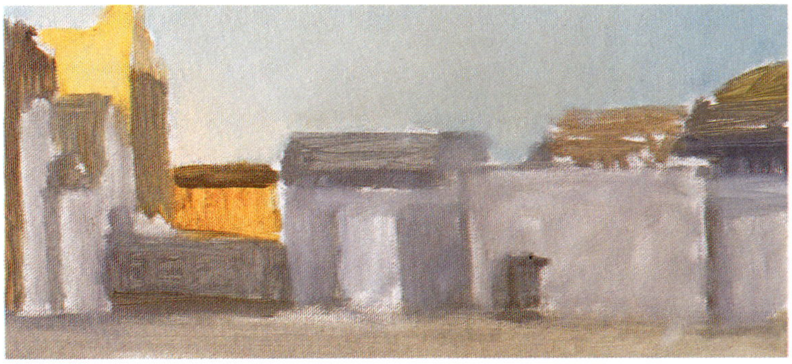

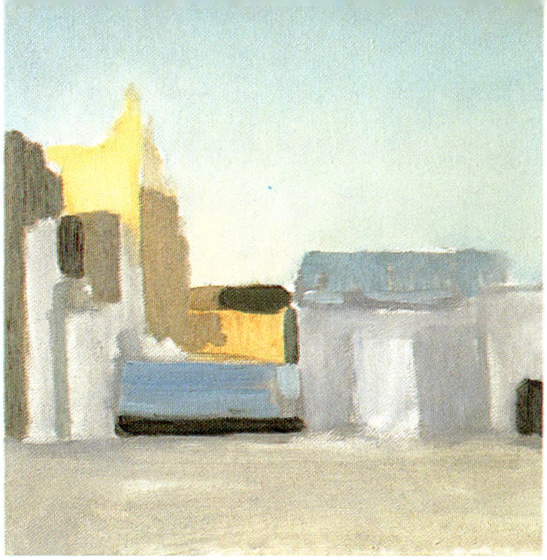

2. The whole of the picture is painted in patches of diluted colors. For the grayest whites, a lot of white is mixed with a little umber and ultramarine. The wall in the foreground is the result of mixing a lot of white with a little ochre and some umber. The warmest colors contain yellow and ochre, yellow and sienna, white and sienna, white and umber. The sky will remain as it is without being retouched. It is Winsor Blue with a lot of white and ochre, to give tone to the brighter areas, and umber to give tone to the darker ones.

3. Now block out the shapes with darker colors to contrast. The mixtures are of ultramarine and umber, or sienna and Winsor Blue and/or ultramarine. In the bluest neutrals, there is more blue and less of the earth colors. The earthy neutrals are a range of earth colors, ochre, sienna, and umber with white as needed.

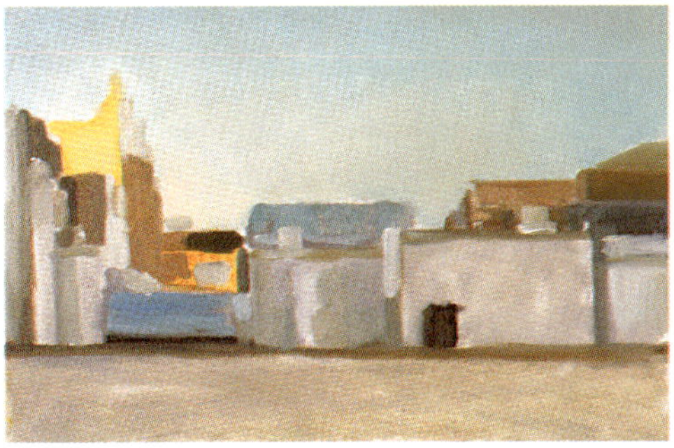

4. Mixtures continue to be applied and adjusted. Use this opportunity to correct outlines and add volume. In short we draw by painting.

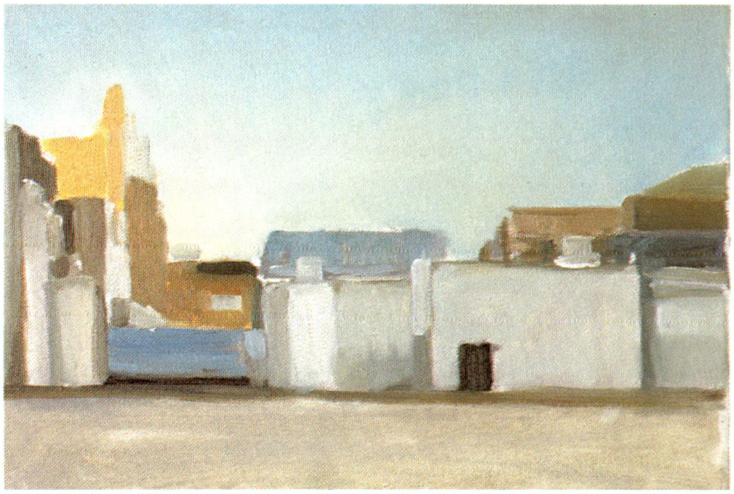

5. Finish off by adding grades of white, giving unity to the white facades. Now darken those areas that look too bright using the lighter neutral colors.

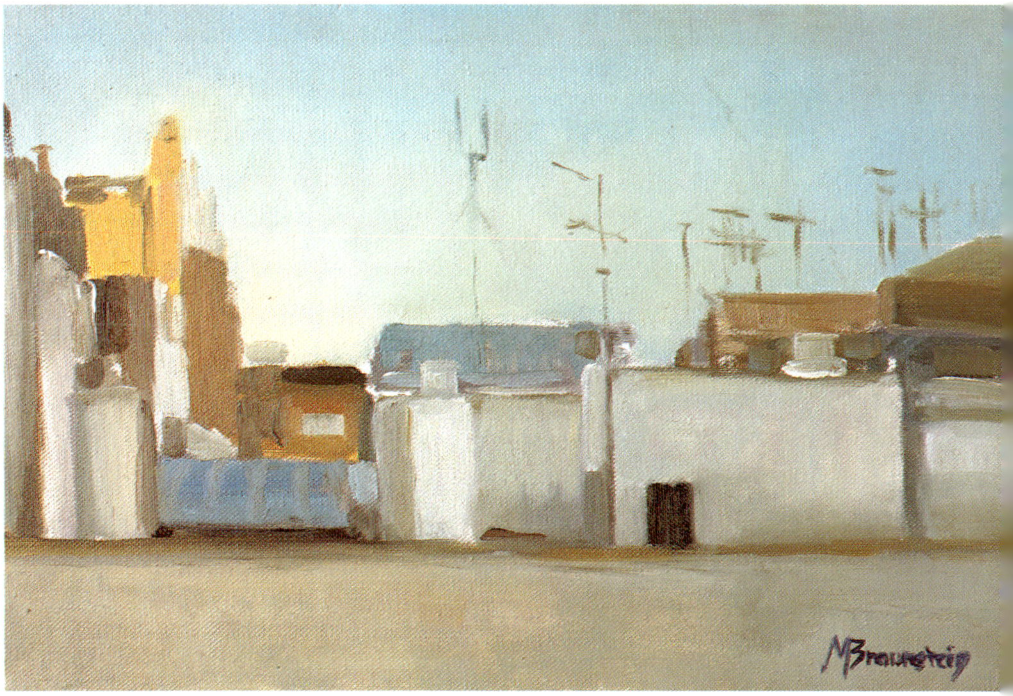

6. Now step back and assess your work. A few more contrasts are added to give a greater sense of volume. A fine paintbrush is used for the final details, such as the aerials. The shape of the blue-colored roof can be emphasized by painting four strips of a lighter shade of blue-gray.

Skin Tones

The figure is bathed in a warm orange light.

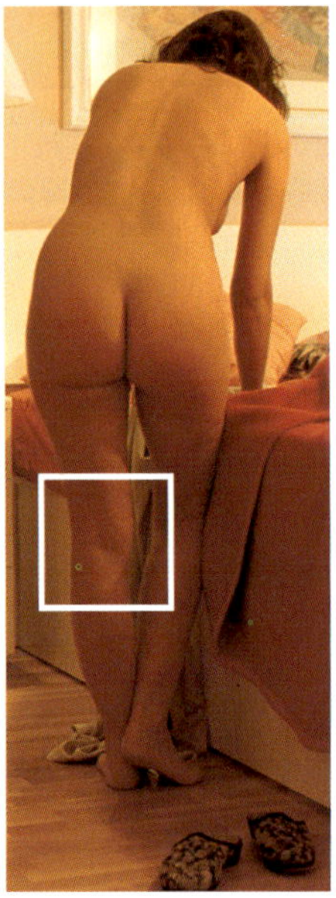

Flesh or skin is full of many different tones and hues. Flesh color depends on the personal characteristics of each individual, combined with the quality of the light falling on it.

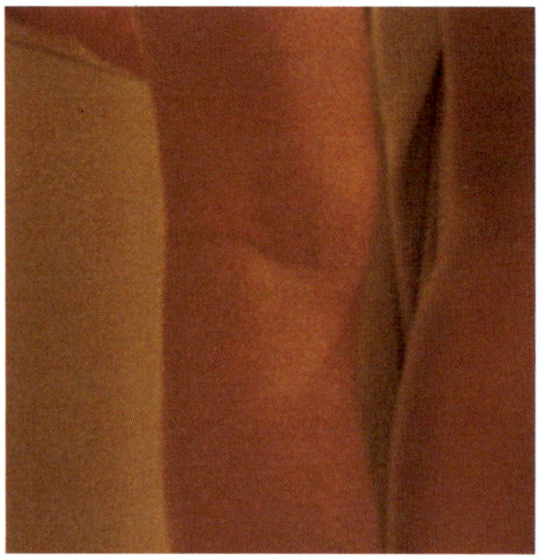

Enlargement of a detail from the model's left leg.

The Palette for Skin Tones

The colors used on the palette depend on the model one is painting. In the first photograph the model's back is bathed in a very warm light, so we will use white, yellow, vermilion, and crimson. The brown color of the model pictured in the second photo is achieved by using earth colors and white, modified with yellow and reddened with vermilion. The cool light in the third example will have an effect on the colors in the skin tones, tending toward ochres and earth colors, earthy and greenish. Basically, the earth colors and white will be used, with occasional toning using Winsor Blue.

Blending the Colors

The skin tones are made lifelike by creating smooth gradations. In the first exercise, the mixtures are laid down with a paintbrush, in adjacent areas of color. Then they are blended with a clean finger. In the area of contact between two colors and different shades, the contrast is made to disappear by strokes of the finger, gradually producing a smooth, progressive gradation.

1. Detail of brushstrokes of the warm tones.

REMEMBER...

- The effect of ochre, when used in mixtures, is to give golden tones, whereas that of sienna is to redden. Umber gives somber tones.
- For very luminous skin tones, yellow, red, and white are used.
- In darker skin tones, and in shadow, blue is added to the mixture.

2. Blending the brushstrokes in 1. In order to compare contrasts, leave some horizontal brushstrokes unblended.

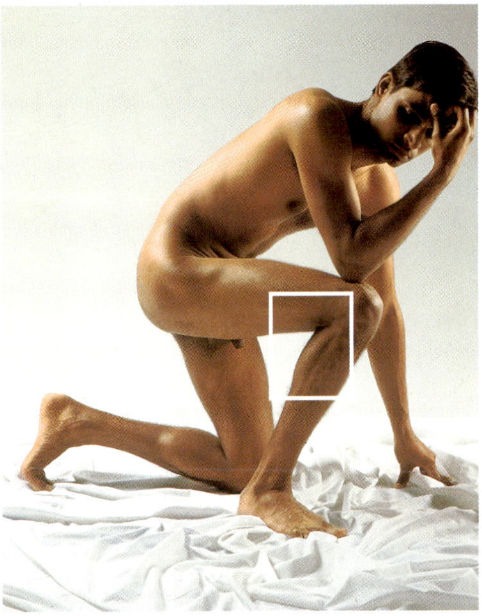

This model's skin is very brown, contrasting strongly in some areas with the light background.

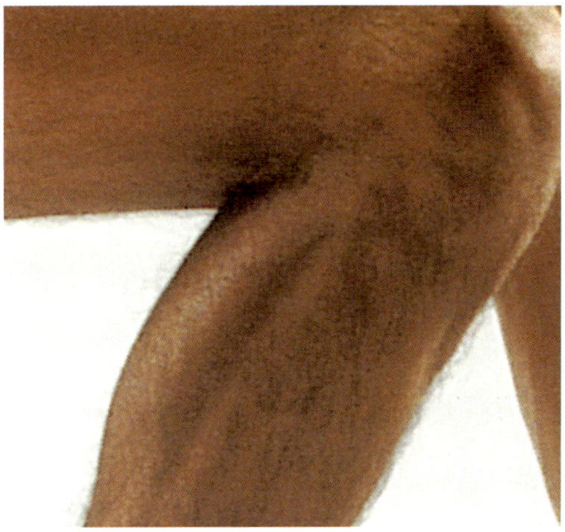

Enlargement of a detail of the right leg.

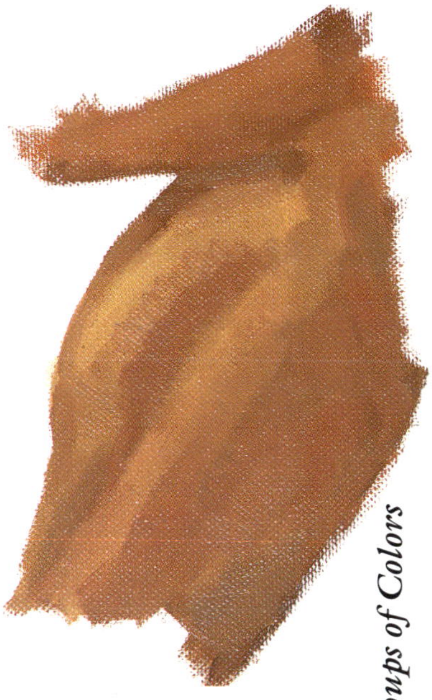

Flesh Tones for Brown Skin

To mix the flesh tones of brown skin, sienna is used as a base. It can be lightened with ochre and white. It is reddened with a slight touch of vermilion. Darkening is done by adding small amounts of umber. In this detail, there are both specific brushstrokes and blended areas.

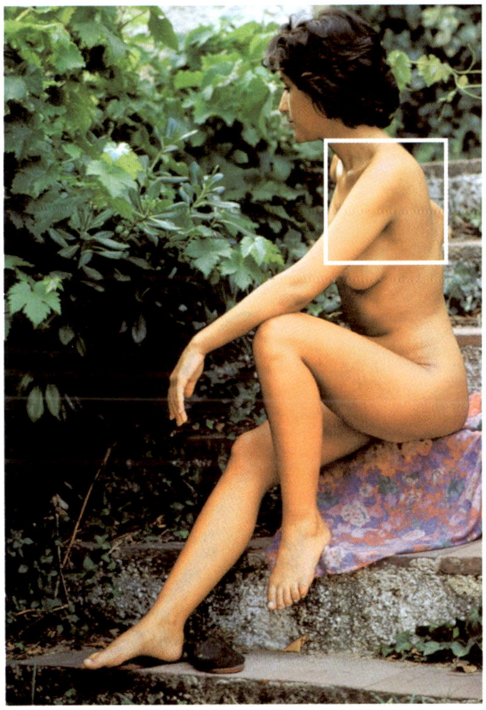

This figure is bathed in a cool light.

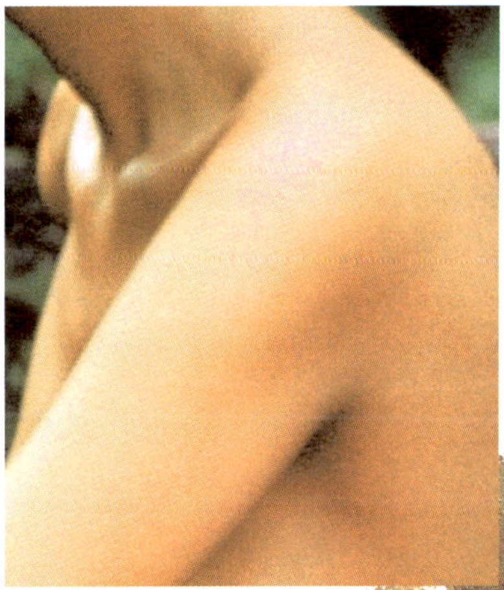

Enlargement of the model's left shoulder.

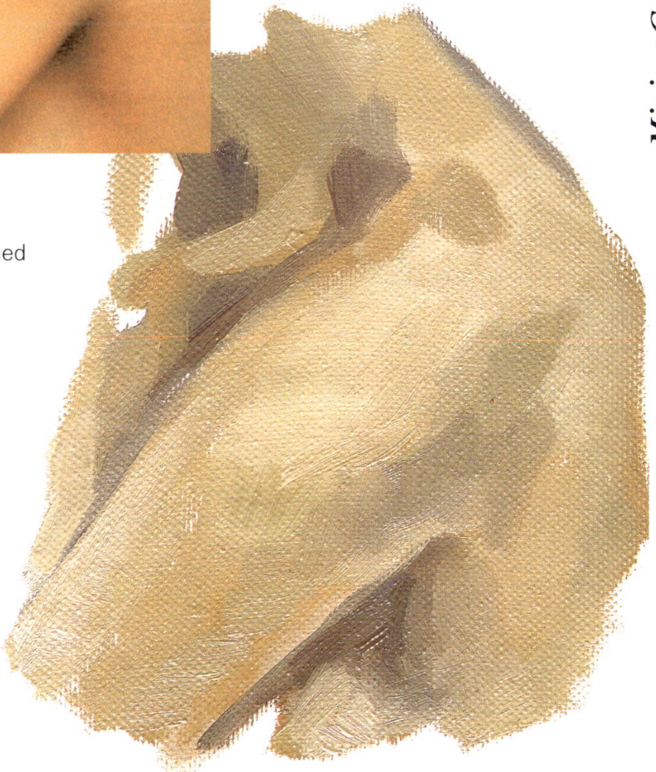

Cool Light

As the model is bathed in a cool light, the mixtures that represent the flesh need to include all three primary colors. They are broken colors, grayish, greenish ochre. Only earth colors are used: ochre, sienna with lots of white. Ochre can be given a blush with a little sienna and plenty of white, aiming for a pallid, broken rosy gray. Umber is present in all the darker mixtures, always for toning and always in small amounts.

Shine and Reflections

Shine and reflections can be seen in any subject with surfaces that reflect both light and the objects that surround it. In order to represent them in paint, mixtures used will generally need to contain a lot of white as well as the hue of the light and objects that reflect it.

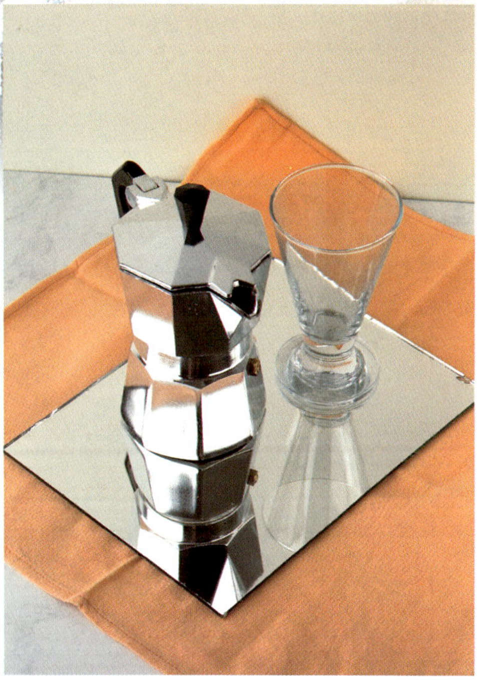

Still life with a lot of shine and reflections. The most suitable palette for painting this model contains the following colors: white, yellow, vermilion, crimson, sienna, Chromium Oxide Green, Winsor Blue, and ultramarine.

Reflecting Surfaces

Every reflecting surface has an intense shine as well as the reflected images of nearby objects. A mirror, glass objects, metals, a great expanse of water, etc..., all have reflecting surfaces.

On other materials, cloths, like silk for example, shades of the colors of nearby objects are registered. Even human skin shines.

The observant artist includes brushstrokes, of all possible tones, to represent shine and reflections. It is one of the keys to reproducing the volume of objects.

REMEMBER...

- In a mixture to represent a very intense shine, a lot of white will be needed.
- In reflected images, along with possible distortion of shapes, the colors of the objects that generate them appear.

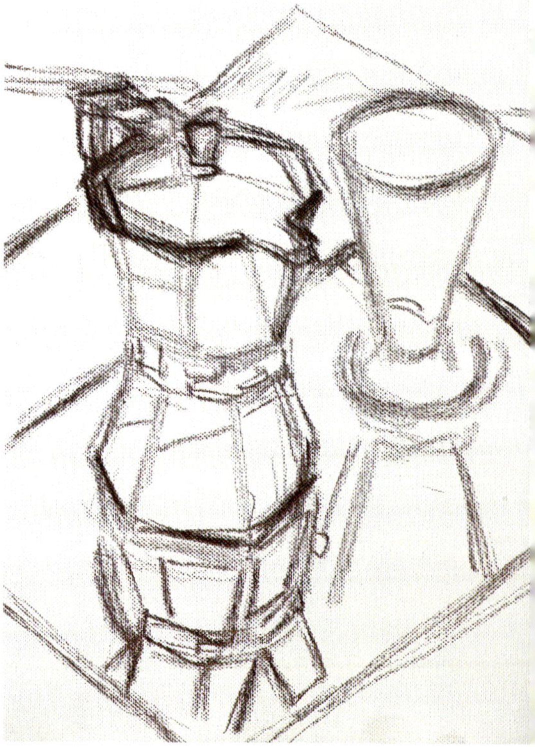

1. In the sketch, lightly drawn lines of charcoal locate the setup on the canvas and outline the most important areas of colors and shades.

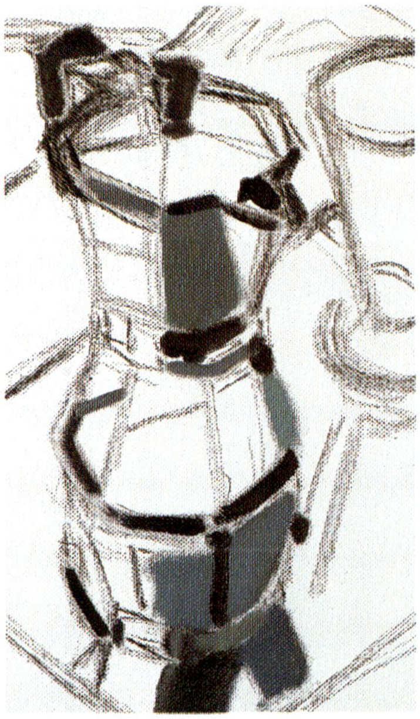

2. For the darkest, almost black, colors, crimson, Chromium Oxide Green, and ultramarine are mixed in approximately equal parts. For the lighter tones, white is gradually added.

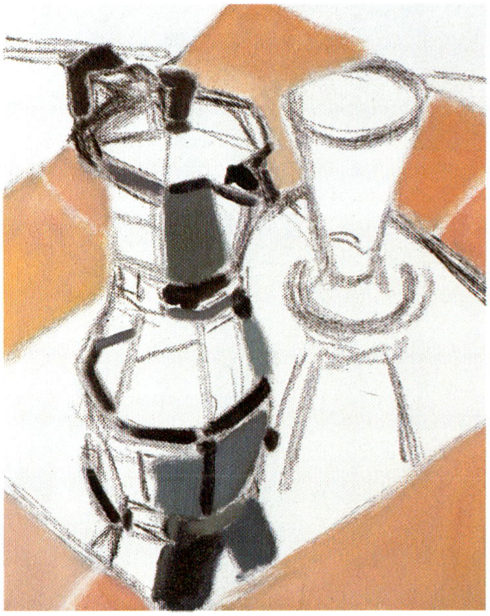

3. The salmon pink of the napkin varies from area to area. In areas of the most orange pink there is somewhat less yellow than vermilion and a lot of white. The most salmon-colored hues are obtained by adding some more crimson to the previous mixture and a touch of sienna.

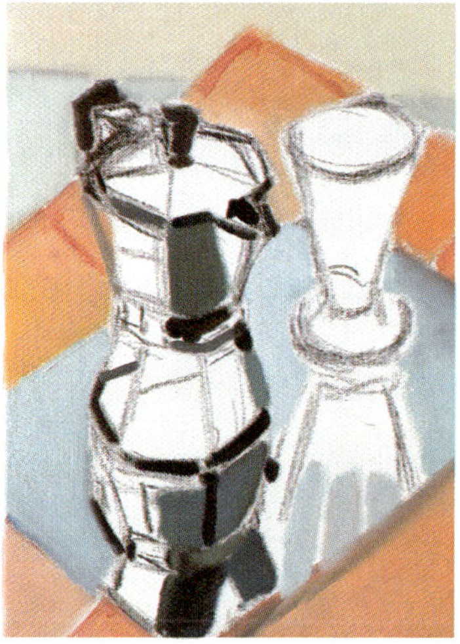

4. The reflections in the mirror have a clear blue-gray hue, as well as some slightly violet tones. Mix Winsor Blue, adding a little yellow and some crimson and, above all, plenty of white. The most violet hue is obtained by adding crimson. The mixture for the wall in the background carries a lot of white, a bit of yellow, a little crimson, and a little Winsor Blue.

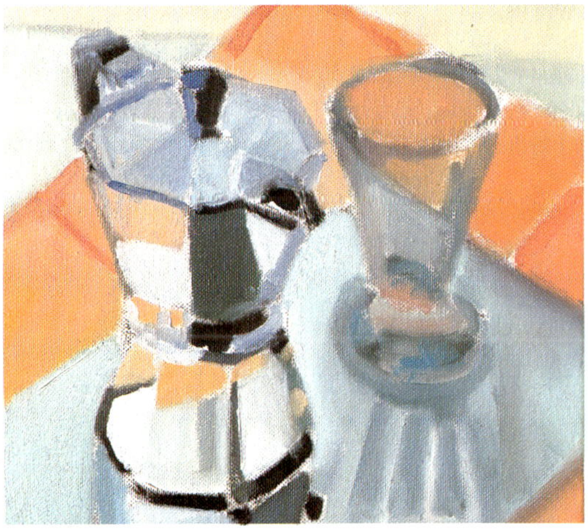

5. Now we continue with the reflections in the coffee pot, the glass, and the mirror. The colors for the salmon pink reflections, in the coffee pot and the glass, are the same mixtures as in 3. For the blue-gray reflections of the coffee pot, the glass, and the mirror, consult the mixtures in 4. Now the paint is left to dry to be resumed in a second session.

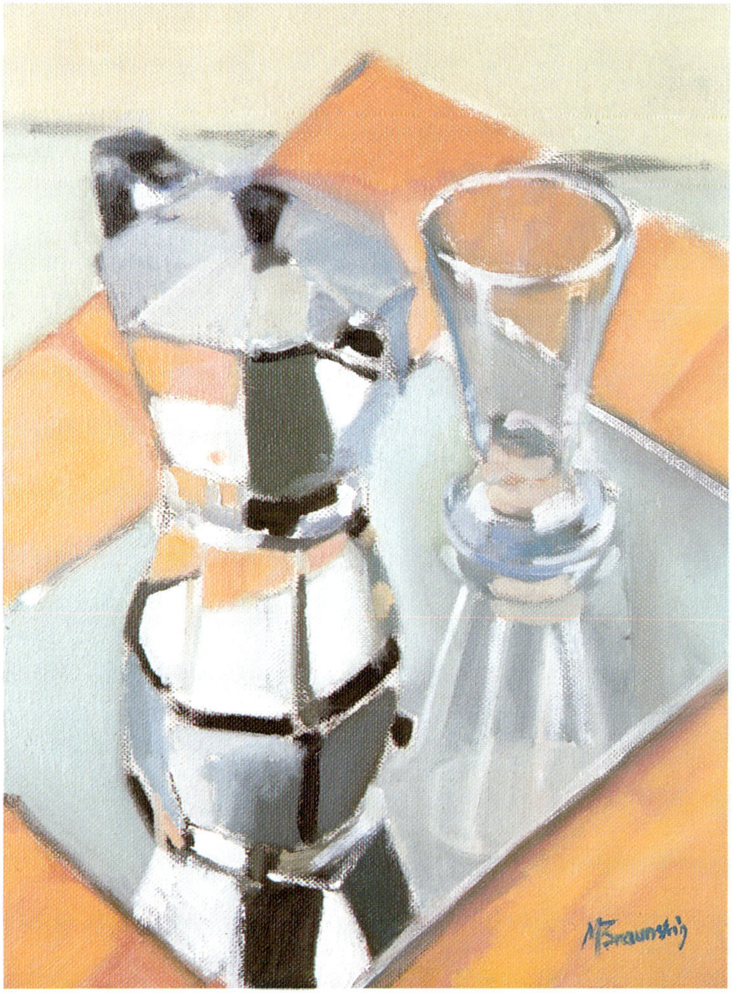

6. In this final step the reflections are finished by adjusting the tones. Use white to retouch the areas of most intense shine, particularly in the coffee pot, the glass, and the mirror. The brightest white has a slight yellowish tinge. This is always an important step for defining glass. Compare the difference between 5 and 6. The brushstrokes for the shine and the reflection in the glass are applied at the last moment and are the lightest.

Painting with Primary Colors and White

Starting from the three primary colors: yellow, crimson, and blue, as well as white, any other color can be created. Painting with just these three colors is an instructive exercise.

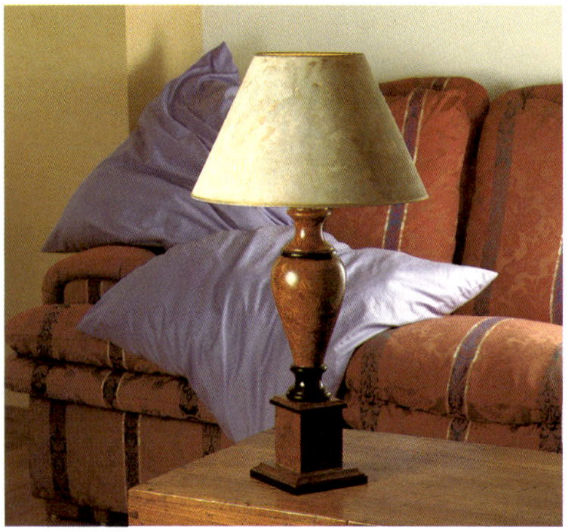

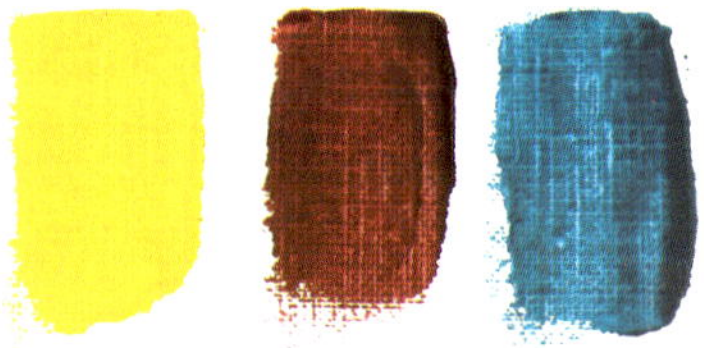

Painting with the Three Primary Colors and White

Let's put into practice a summary of all you have learned. Use your knowledge of the proportions of the primaries to obtain secondaries and tertiaries, what you know about lightening and darkening a color, and the precautions to take with mixtures of complementary colors.

In this exercise, carried out in several sessions, a distinction will be made among three groups of mixtures. Those related to the sofa consist of lightening and darkening crimson. The cushions will require the lightening and darkening of blue. Except for the colors of the wall in the background, and the sofa and the cushions, the rest are neutral earth colors.

In the first layer, which is shown in step 2, the sofa is painted in crimson and the cushions in Winsor Blue with the addition of a small amount of crimson. The reddish ochre is a mixture of yellow, somewhat less crimson, and very little blue. The color similar to sienna is a mixture of yellow and crimson in equal parts plus a little Winsor Blue. The lightest earth tone is obtained by diluting a lot of crimson, a little yellow, and hardly any blue. The shadowed areas of the lampshade are painted with bluish gray. You can make this up from Winsor Blue, very little crimson, a slight touch of yellow, and a lot of white.

REMEMBER...

- The amount of each color used in a mixture will determine depth of shades and hues.
- By gradually adjusting the mixtures and amounts, you can approximate the colors of your subject.

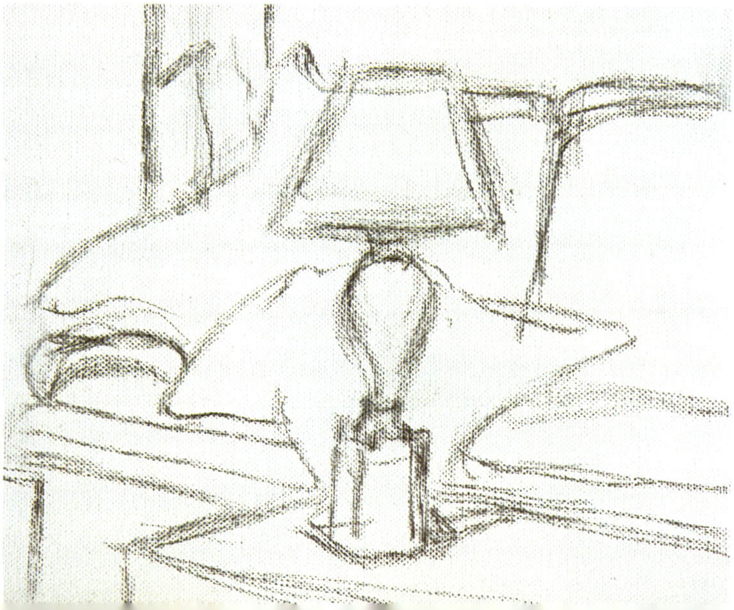

1. In the sketch, which is drawn in charcoal, only the principal lines of the composition are blocked in. The lamp is nearly centered.

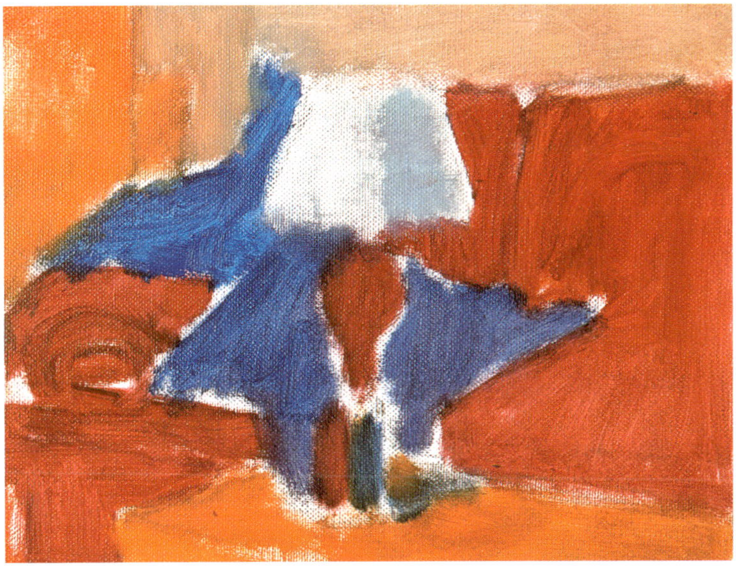

2. The first layer is applied with the paint diluted. A cotton rag is used to remove excess paint while it is still wet, in order to block in areas for colors and tones.

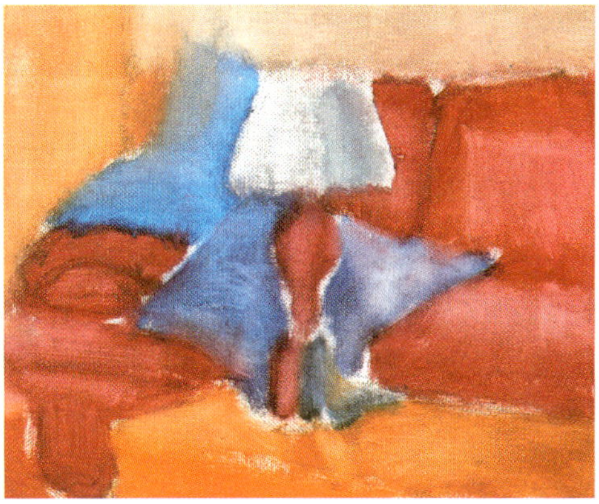

3. Now define the background. The broken white of the wall in the background is the same mixture as for the shadow on the lampshade, but with more white. Keep adjusting your tones and colors. For the earthy walls in the background the golden hue is obtained with a lot of yellow, some crimson and hardly any blue, and a lot of white. The most salmon-colored pink is crimson and yellow in equal parts, very little blue, and a lot of white.

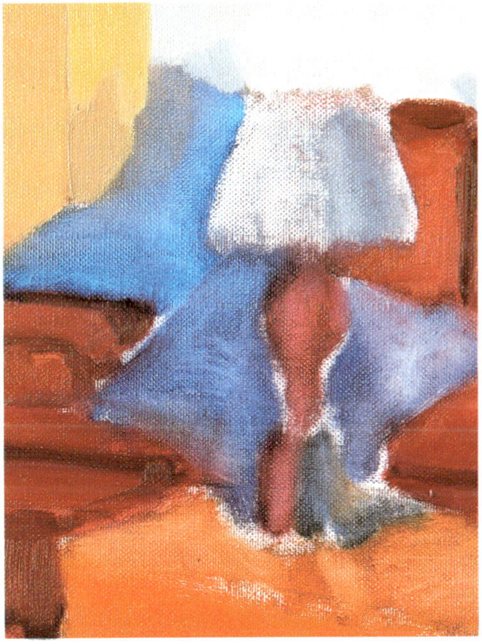

5. In the cushions, tones appear that reflect the sofa and the light as well as deepening into cast shadows. A mixture of the three primaries, with a bluish tone, can be used: 50% blue, 25% crimson, and 25% yellow, lightened with white for gradations.

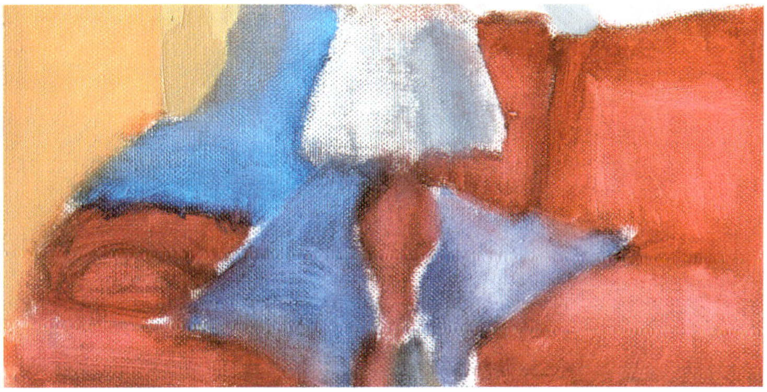

4. The color of the sofa is achieved by lightening the crimson with a little yellow to make it a crimson red. Add a little white in the more illuminated areas. The crimson is darkened with a little blue for the contrasts.

6. Lastly, the lamp and the table in the foreground are finished. The color for the table is a mixture of crimson, somewhat less yellow and very little blue, and some white. The shadowed area of the lampshade is finished with a glaze of white. The lightest part is finished off with white, given warmth with a little yellow.

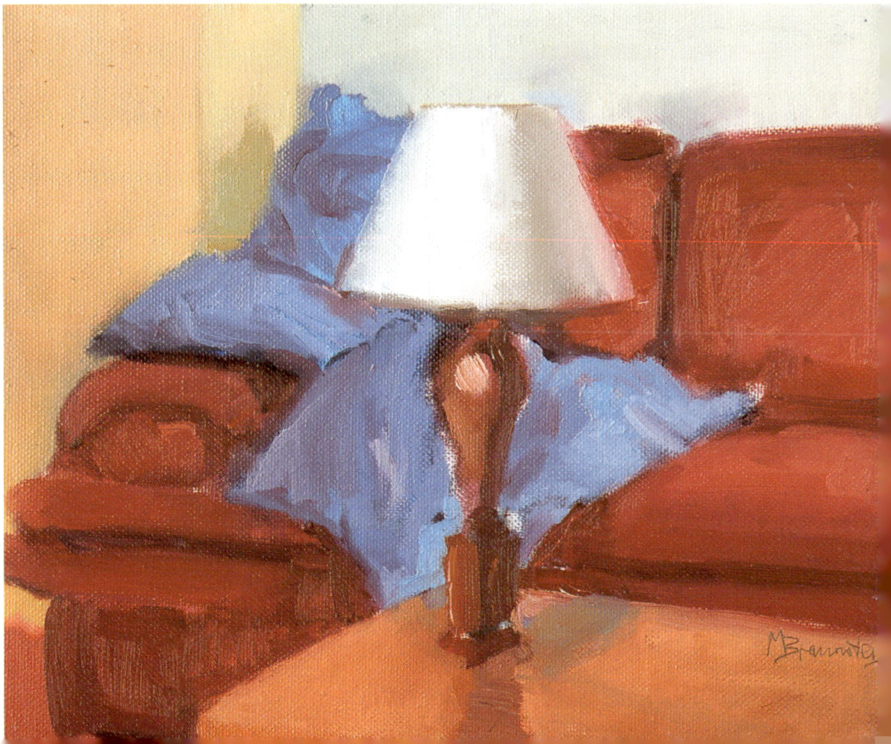